Copyright © 2012
Disciple Maker Ministries

All rights reserved.

No part of this book may be reproduced in any form without written permission from the author or publisher, except for the inclusion of brief quotations in a review.

Dr. Lance T. Ketchum
A.B.S., Th.B., Th.M., Ph.D.

First Printing -April 2012

Handfuls on Purpose

List Price: **$15.95 each**
plus postage and handling

ISBN 978-0-9860113-1-3

DISCOUNTS ARE AVAILABLE FOR QUANTITY ORDERS
CHECK WEB-SITE FOR PRICING

Additional copies can be obtained from

Disciple Maker Ministries

224 Fifth Avenue N.W.
Hutchinson, Minnesota 55350

612-750-5515

E-Mail: LanceKetchum@msn.com

www.disciplemakerministries.org

TABLE OF CONTENTS

Chapter	Chapter Subject	Page
	Introduction and Overview	4
One	Running Away from God	16
Two	Learning to Fear the Lord	23
Three	Removing the Blinders to Time to See the Blessings of Eternity	33
Four	Six Resolutions of Spiritual Commitment to Sanctification	42
Five	Full Surrender: the Open Door to Power with God	54
Six	The Pathway of Blessing Through the Graveyard of Pride	65
Seven	Christ: Our Kinsman Redeemer	74
Eight	Seven Character Traits of a Person with a Servant's Heart	82
Nine	Understanding the Value of Holiness and Commitment	92
Ten	Finding Grace	101
Eleven	The God of Love and Grace and The Work Of Grace	108
Twelve	The Security of God's Protection in the Center of His Will	117
Thirteen	Dealing with Conflict and Problems God's Way	125
Fourteen	Gleaning in the Field of God's Love	134
Fifteen	Understanding the Seasons of the Soul	143
Sixteen	Claiming Redemption by Claiming Our Redeemer	151
Seventeen	The Miracle of Redemption	158
Eighteen	The Redeemer that cannot Redeem	165
Nineteen	The Shoeless Redeemer	173
Twenty	That the Name of the Dead Be Not Cut Off	180
Twenty-one	The Resurrection of The Bride of Christ	188
Twenty-two	The Restoration of the Nation Of Israel	196
	Lexicons and Dictionaries	204

Handfuls On Purpose
Studies in the Book of Ruth
Introduction and Overview
(Please read this overview before studying the lessons.)

Welcome to the study of the book of Ruth. Great things sometimes come in small packages. Such is the case with the little book of Ruth. The time you spend in the book of Ruth may prove to be one of the greatest investments of your life. It is God's love story to humanity. The setting for the book of Ruth is "in the days when the judges ruled."

"<u>Now it came to pass in the days when the judges ruled</u>, that there was a famine in the land. And a certain man of Bethlehemjudah went to sojourn in the country of Moab, he, and his wife, and his two sons" (Ruth 1:1).

During this period, God intended the nation of Israel to function as a Theocracy. God was to be their King and was to govern them through His Law and through various "Judges" who He raised up to deliver Israel from the consequences of her rebellion against God's Law. It is apparent that these people did not want a heavenly King, but a king "like other nations."

"[4] Then all the elders of Israel gathered themselves together, and came to Samuel unto Ramah, [5] And said unto him, Behold, thou art old, and thy sons walk not in thy ways: <u>now make us a king to judge us like all the nations.</u> [6] But the thing displeased Samuel, when they said, Give us a king to judge us. And Samuel prayed unto the LORD" (I Samuel 8:4-6).

The days of the Judges were, in most part, very dark days for the nation of Israel. The sin cycle continued to repeat itself with each succeeding generation. With each generation, there was a gradual and progressive movement away from obedience to the Word of God and of worship in truth.

Each new generation grew weaker and weaker, becoming more and more a nation of spiritual sickness and consumption (as typified by the two sons of Naomi, Mahlon and Chilion). Israel was very much like the Church of today. They wanted God's blessing and provision for them, but not His authority over them or any responsibility to Him. They wanted a *distant* God when it came to their unfaithful practices, but a *near* God when it came to their wants and needs.

We find this great contrast in what is represented by the name Elimelech in Ruth 1:1 and the last verse of the book of Judges. The name Elimelech means, "God is my King."

> "In those days *there was* no king in Israel: every man did *that which was* right in his own eyes" (Judges 21:25).

In Ruth 1:1-5, we see the consequences of that attitude.

> "¹ Now it came to pass in the days when the judges ruled, that there was a famine in the land. And a certain man of Bethlehemjudah went to sojourn in the country of Moab, he, and his wife, and his two sons. ² And the name of the man *was* Elimelech, and the name of his wife Naomi, and the name of his two sons Mahlon and Chilion, Ephrathites of Bethlehemjudah. And they came into the country of Moab, and continued there. ³ And Elimelech Naomi's husband died; and she was left, and her two sons. ⁴ And they took them wives of the women of Moab; the name of the one *was* Orpah, and the name of the other Ruth: and they dwelled there about ten years. ⁵ And Mahlon and Chilion died also both of them; and the woman was left of her two sons and her husband."

The fact that Elimelech left Bethlehem with the intention of finding food and staying for only a short time ("sojourn," v. 1) is not the problem. The problem is that it was an attempt to escape the chastisement of the LORD. That is not possible. When a believer moves away from God's absolutes, judgment and chastisement will come. They are inevitable because in suffering and hopelessness people will cry out to God. That is God's purpose in chastisement. God's goodness leads sinners to repentance (Romans 2:4).

The days of the Judges were a history of failure through compromise and complacency. It is in this black, sinful historical setting that God records the story of Ruth - the story of His redeeming love. This is God's love story for His creation written in white chalk on a *blackboard of sin*.

In Ruth 1:1, God draws our attention to the little town of Bethlehem in the land of the tribe of Judah. The name Bethlehem-

Judah literally translated means the "house of bread" in the land of "praise." However, in this day of Israel's history, there was no bread in the house of bread, nor praise in the land of praise.

To a people living for themselves and not for the LORD, God necessitates a famine to show the spiritual famine in the land. God wanted them to know that they were starving themselves spiritually. Instead of recognizing the problem and repenting, Elimelech and his family leave the "house of bread" in the land of praise and head for Moab. Moab was the sewer, the spiritual cesspool, of the area.

> "Moab *is* my washpot; over Edom will I cast out my shoe; over Philistia will I triumph" (Psalms 108:9).

The word "washpot" in Psalm 108:9 means a *boiling cauldron for cleansing.* Moab was to be used of God as a *cleansing place* - a place where God would bring Israel (typified by Naomi) face to face with the cause of her chastisement.

What God wanted of Israel was for them to change the *way* they lived. Instead, they ran away from God's chastisement and only changed the *place* they lived. Changing their place would not change their ways, because they had not changed their relationship with the Lord or their attitude towards Him. They needed a change of heart, not just a change of place.

In the book of Ruth, Naomi represents the nation of Israel. Elimelech, her husband, whose name means "God is my King," represents the testimony of Israel to the world. However, that testimony was made at total contradiction by the way Israel lived *before the world* and *in the world*. Therefore, they destroyed their testimony and Elimelech died.

What we fail to see so often in the typology of Ruth is that Naomi (Israel) was spiritually unfaithful to her husband (God) and her testimony (God is my King). She proclaimed God to be her King, yet the world was her lover. God summed up the attitude and actions of Israel in Ezekiel 16:22-32, and the people with which they unfaithfully chose to inhabit the Land:

> "[22] And in all thine abominations and thy whoredoms thou hast not remembered the days of thy youth, when thou wast naked and bare, *and* wast polluted in thy blood. [23] And it came to pass after all thy

wickedness, (woe, woe unto thee! saith the Lord GOD;)²⁴ *That* thou hast also built unto thee an eminent place, and hast made thee an high place in every street. ²⁵ Thou hast built thy high place at every head of the way, and hast made thy beauty to be abhorred, and hast opened thy feet to every one that passed by, and multiplied thy whoredoms. ²⁶ Thou hast also committed fornication with the Egyptians thy neighbours, great of flesh; and hast increased thy whoredoms, to provoke me to anger. ²⁷ Behold, therefore I have stretched out my hand over thee, and have diminished thine ordinary *food*, and delivered thee unto the will of them that hate thee, the daughters of the Philistines, which are ashamed of thy lewd way. ²⁸ Thou hast played the whore also with the Assyrians, because thou wast unsatiable; yea, thou hast played the harlot with them, and yet couldest not be satisfied. ²⁹ Thou hast moreover multiplied thy fornication in the land of Canaan unto Chaldea; and yet thou wast not satisfied herewith. ³⁰ How weak is thine heart, saith the Lord GOD, seeing thou doest all these *things*, the work of an imperious whorish woman; ³¹ In that thou buildest thine eminent place in the head of every way, and makest thine high place in every street; and hast not been as an harlot, in that thou scornest hire; ³² *But as* a wife that committeth adultery, *which* taketh strangers instead of her husband" (Ezekiel 16:22-32)!

In order to understand the book of Ruth it is necessary to understand the biblical concept of the Kinsman Redeemer. Lewis Sperry Chafer says the following:

". . . (c) a lost estate could be redeemed by a kinsman (Lev.25:25). This practice becomes a type of Christ's redemption. There were four requirements in the type as likewise four antitype; (1) A redeemer must be a near kinsman. To fulfill this Christ took upon Himself the human form, entered the race. (2) He must be able to redeem. The price of redemption must needs be paid, which in antitype was the blood of the Son of God (Acts 20:28; I Peter 1:18-19). (3) He must be willing to redeem (cf. Heb. 10:4-10). (4) He must be free from the calamity which occasioned the need of redemption, that is to say, he could not redeem himself. This was true of Christ, for He needed no redemption. According to the type of the high priest on the Day of Atonement, then, Christ offered sacrifice but not for Himself (Luke 1:35; Heb. 4:15)."[1]

---

[1] Chafer, Lewis Sperry. *Systematic Theology.* Vol. VII. Dallas: Dallas Seminary Press, 1976, 263-264.

In the Old Covenant, the concept of the Kinsman Redeemer relates mostly to the care of widows or children that had lost a husband or sons. The concept of the Kinsman Redeemer was to insure that property designated to one tribe remained within that tribe. The women would not be able to care for themselves or take care of the land in such a hostile environment. When a Kinsman redeemed his near kin's property, he also redeemed his kin's family and cared for them as his own. This view considered a man's wife(s) and children to be his possessions. The Levitical Law was specific about these matters.

"[25] If thy brother be waxen poor, and hath sold away *some* of his possession, and if any of his kin come to redeem it, then shall he redeem that which his brother sold. [26] And if the man have none to redeem it, and himself be able to redeem it; [27] Then let him count the years of the sale thereof, and restore the overplus unto the man to whom he sold it; that he may return unto his possession. [28] But if he be not able to restore *it* to him, then that which is sold shall remain in the hand of him that hath bought it until the year of jubile: and in the jubile it shall go out, and he shall return unto his possession. [29] And if a man sell a dwelling house in a walled city, then he may redeem it within a whole year after it is sold; *within* a full year may he redeem it. [30] And if it be not redeemed within the space of a full year, then the house that *is* in the walled city shall be established for ever to him that bought it throughout his generations: it shall not go out in the jubile. [31] But the houses of the villages which have no wall round about them shall be counted as the fields of the country: they may be redeemed, and they shall go out in the jubile. [32] Notwithstanding the cities of the Levites, *and* the houses of the cities of their possession, may the Levites redeem at any time. [33] And if a man purchase of the Levites, then the house that was sold, and the city of his possession, shall go out in *the year of* jubile: for the houses of the cities of the Levites *are* their possession among the children of Israel. [34] But the field of the suburbs of their cities may not be sold; for it *is* their perpetual possession. [35] And if thy brother be waxen poor, and fallen in decay with thee; then thou shalt relieve him: *yea, though he be* a stranger, or a sojourner; that he may live with thee. [36] Take thou no usury of him, or increase: but fear thy God; that thy brother may live with thee. [37] Thou shalt not give him thy money upon usury, nor lend him thy victuals for increase. [38] I *am* the LORD your God, which brought you forth out of the land of Egypt, to give you the land of Canaan, *and* to be your

God. ⁳⁹ And if thy brother *that dwelleth* by thee be waxen poor, and be sold unto thee; thou shalt not compel him to serve as a bondservant: ⁴⁰ *But* as an hired servant, *and* as a sojourner, he shall be with thee, *and* shall serve thee unto the year of jubile: ⁴¹ And *then* shall he depart from thee, *both* he and his children with him, and shall return unto his own family, and unto the possession of his fathers shall he return. ⁴² For they *are* my servants, which I brought forth out of the land of Egypt: they shall not be sold as bondmen. ⁴³ Thou shalt not rule over him with rigour; but shalt fear thy God. ⁴⁴ Both thy bondmen, and thy bondmaids, which thou shalt have, *shall be* of the heathen that are round about you; of them shall ye buy bondmen and bondmaids. ⁴⁵ Moreover of the children of the strangers that do sojourn among you, of them shall ye buy, and of their families that *are* with you, which they begat in your land: and they shall be your possession. ⁴⁶ And ye shall take them as an inheritance for your children after you, to inherit *them for* a possession; they shall be your bondmen for ever: but over your brethren the children of Israel, ye shall not rule one over another with rigour. ⁴⁷ And if a sojourner or stranger wax rich by thee, and thy brother *that dwelleth* by him wax poor, and sell himself unto the stranger *or* sojourner by thee, or to the stock of the stranger's family: ⁴⁸ After that he is sold he may be redeemed again; one of his brethren may redeem him: ⁴⁹ Either his uncle, or his uncle's son, may redeem him, or *any* that is nigh of kin unto him of his family may redeem him; or if he be able, he may redeem himself. ⁵⁰ And he shall reckon with him that bought him from the year that he was sold to him unto the year of jubile: and the price of his sale shall be according unto the number of years, according to the time of an hired servant shall it be with him. ⁵¹ If *there be* yet many years *behind*, according unto them he shall give again the price of his redemption out of the money that he was bought for. ⁵² And if there remain but few years unto the year of jubile, then he shall count with him, *and* according unto his years shall he give him again the price of his redemption. ⁵³ *And* as a yearly hired servant shall he be with him: *and the other* shall not rule with rigour over him in thy sight. ⁵⁴ And if he be not redeemed in these *years*, then he shall go out in the year of jubile, *both* he, and his children with him. ⁵⁵ For unto me the children of Israel *are* servants; they *are* my servants whom I brought forth out of the land of Egypt: I *am* the LORD your God" (Leviticus 25:25-55).

Another responsibility of the Kinsman Redeemer was to marry the widow of a dead kinsman that was without a son, and to carry on his father's name. He was to marry her and raise the children to testify to the dead man's name.

> "[5] If brethren dwell together, and one of them die, and have no child, the wife of the dead shall not marry without unto a stranger: her husband's brother shall go in unto her, and take her to him to wife, and perform the duty of an husband's brother unto her. [6] And it shall be, *that* the firstborn which she beareth shall succeed in the name of his brother *which is* dead, that his name be not put out of Israel. [7] And if the man like not to take his brother's wife, then let his brother's wife go up to the gate unto the elders, and say, My husband's brother refuseth to raise up unto his brother a name in Israel, he will not perform the duty of my husband's brother. [8] Then the elders of his city shall call him, and speak unto him: and *if* he stand *to it*, and say, I like not to take her; [9] Then shall his brother's wife come unto him in the presence of the elders, and loose his shoe from off his foot, and spit in his face, and shall answer and say, So shall it be done unto that man that will not build up his brother's house. [10] And his name shall be called in Israel, The house of him that hath his shoe loosed" (Deuteronomy 25:5-10).

This text of the Law would play a big part in the story of Ruth as detailed in Ruth 4:5:

> "Then said Boaz, What day thou buyest the field of the hand of Naomi, thou must buy *it* also of Ruth the Moabitess, the wife of the dead, to raise up the name of the dead upon his inheritance" (Ruth 4:5).

The typology existing between Boaz and the Lord Jesus Christ is also significant to understanding the book of Ruth. The Scofield Study Bible has the following note on Isaiah 59:20:

> "Redemption: Kinsman type, summary. The goel, or Kinsman-Redeemer, is a beautiful type of Christ. (1) The kinsman redemption was of persons, and an inheritance (Lev. 25:48; 25:25; Gal. 4:5; Eph. 1:7, 11, 14). (2) The Redeemer must be a kinsman (Lev. 25:48-49; Ruth 3:12-13; Gal. 4:4; Heb. 2:14-15). (3) The Redeemer must be able to redeem (Ruth 4:4-6; Jer. 50:34; John 10:11, 18). (4) Redemption is effected by the goel paying the just

demand in full (Lev.25:27; 1 Pet. 1:18-19; Gal. 3:13)."[2]

The Lord Jesus Christ fulfills the spiritual reality of which Boaz is the type. As detailed in the Scofield notes, Jesus fulfills each of the Law's demands of a Kinsman Redeemer. Yet there are aspects of the type in Boaz that go beyond the expectations of the Law. Boaz's love for Ruth reveals these aspects as well as the grace by which he ministers the Law to her and to Naomi. Christ came in love and in grace to redeem lost sinners.

"[16] For God so loved the world, that he gave his only begotten Son, that whosoever believeth in him should not perish, but have everlasting life. [17] For God sent not his Son into the world to condemn the world; but that the world through him might be saved. [18] He that believeth on him is not condemned: but he that believeth not is condemned already, because he hath not believed in the name of the only begotten Son of God" (John 3:16-18).

"[8] For by grace are ye saved through faith; and that not of yourselves: *it is* the gift of God: [9] Not of works, lest any man should boast. [10] For we are his workmanship, created in Christ Jesus unto good works, which God hath before ordained that we should walk in them" (Ephesians 2:8-10).

In the Old Testament, poverty usually resulted in bondage to a master who would require redemption from that bondage. In the New Testament, God portrays the sinner as being bankrupt of righteousness. God portrays the sinner in bondage to the corruption of sin and cursed by the Law. Christ redeems believing humanity from the curse of the Law.

"Christ hath redeemed us from the curse of the law, being made a curse for us: for it is written, Cursed *is* every one that hangeth on a tree:. ." (Galatians 3:13).

In doing so, He bought sinners out of the *market place of the corruption of sin* and brought them into His family declaring them to be adult children of God.

---

[2] Scofield, C.I. *The Scofield Study Bible*. New York: Oxford Press, 1996.

"For we know that the law is spiritual: but I am carnal, sold under sin" (Romans 7:14).

"To redeem them that were under the law, that we might receive the adoption of sons" (Galatians 4:5).

Love is willing to pay any price necessary to redeem the person loved.

"Greater love hath no man than this, that a man lay down his life for his friends" (John 15:13).

The degree of Christ's love for lost humanity is measured by the price He was willing to pay to redeem them.

"[9] And they sung a new song, saying, Thou art worthy to take the book, and to open the seals thereof: for thou wast slain, and hast <u>redeemed us to God by thy blood</u> out of every kindred, and tongue, and people, and nation; [10] And hast made us unto our God kings and priests: and we shall reign on the earth" (Revelation 5:9-10).

"Take heed therefore unto yourselves, and to all the flock, over the which the Holy Ghost hath made you overseers, to feed the church of God, <u>which he hath purchased with his own blood</u>" (Acts 20:28).

The type represented by Boaz is temporal and physical in its ramifications while the reality in Christ is eternal and Soteriological in its application.

"[19] What? know ye not that your body is the temple of the Holy Ghost *which is* in you, which ye have of God, and ye are not your own? [20] <u>For ye are bought with a price: therefore glorify God in your body, and in your spirit, which are God's</u>" (I Corinthians 6: 19-20).

"[22] For he that is called in the Lord, *being* a servant, is the Lord's freeman: likewise also he that is called, *being* free, is Christ's servant. [23] <u>Ye are bought with a price; be not ye the servants of men</u>" (I Corinthians 7:22-23).

"Who gave himself for us, that he might redeem us from all iniquity, and purify unto himself a peculiar people, zealous of good works" (Titus 2:14).

"*¹⁸* Forasmuch as ye know that ye were not redeemed with corruptible things, *as* silver and gold, from your vain conversation *received* by tradition from your fathers; *¹⁹* But with the precious blood of Christ, as of a lamb without blemish and without spot: . . ." (I Peter 1:18-19).

"Being justified freely by his grace through the redemption that is in Christ Jesus: . . " (Romans 3:24).

Just as the *safe shelter* of the strength of Boaz's household gave Ruth and Naomi security for the balance of their lives, so does the strength of Christ's "household" give His redeemed eternal security.

"*²⁸* And I give unto them eternal life; and they shall never perish, neither shall any *man* pluck them out of my hand. *²⁹* My Father, which gave *them* me, is greater than all; and no *man* is able to pluck *the*] out of my Father's hand. *³⁰* I and *my* Father are one" (John 10:28-30).

"Jude, the servant of Jesus Christ, and brother of James, to them that are sanctified by God the Father, and preserved in Jesus Christ, *and* called:" (Jude 1:1).

We can say that the book of Ruth is like a play written in four acts. Act I begins with a man named Elimelech of the tribe of Judah in the city of Bethlehem in the land of Judah. There was famine in the land of Judah, so Elimelech takes his wife Naomi, their two sons, Mahlon and Chilion, to Moab with the intent of staying for a short time until the famine is over. While the family is in Moab, Elimelech dies. Shortly thereafter, his two sons take two Moabite women to be their wives. Mahlon marries Ruth and Chilion marries her sister Orpah. Then, after about ten years, the two sons die.

Naomi hears that the famine in Judah is over and decides to return home. Ruth and Orpah begin the journey with her. After Naomi considers the poverty waiting for her at Bethlehem, she encourages her daughters-in-law to return to their mother's house. After considerable discussion of the matter, Orpah decides to return while Ruth vows to remain with Naomi regardless of the cost.

At the end of Act I they arrive in Bethlehem, where the

women of the city gather around Naomi in amazement at her loss. Naomi publicly recognizes her loss and the chastisement of God. She reflects that her life is no longer *pleasant*, but now very *bitter*. Therefore, she instructs the women to call her "Mara" meaning *bitter*, rather than "Naomi," which means *pleasant*. Naomi and Ruth arrive in Jerusalem at the beginning of barley harvest, which lasted about seven to ten days. Acts II and III take place during those few days of barley harvest.

In Act II Boaz is introduced as a "kinsman" of Elimelech. He is a man with a strong house and considerable wealth. Ruth begins to glean in his field during the harvest of the barley, where she first makes his acquaintance. Boaz inquires of his servants as to who Ruth is. He apparently recognizes that she is part of his family and begins to make provision for her protection and care. Boaz invites Ruth to eat with his reapers where he personally passes her the *roasted grain* to eat, making her feel welcome. Boaz gives instruction to his *young men* to give Ruth special privileges, even to drop some "handfuls on purpose" for her to recover.

At the close of Act II, Ruth returns to the city of Bethlehem and to Naomi with her day's bounty. She informs Naomi of her encounter with Boaz and his provision for her. Ruth continues gleaning in the fields of Boaz under his provisions throughout the barley harvest and the wheat harvest.

In Act III, we find Naomi and Ruth preparing to claim Boaz as Kinsman Redeemer. Boaz was *winnowing barley* at the "threshingfloor." The "threshingfloor" was a hard-parched clay circular on top of a hill. In the late afternoon, a breeze would begin to blow and threshing and winnowing would begin. As long as the wind blew, the threshing continued. It often continued late into the night and early morning.

It would appear from Ruth 3:1-4 that Boaz was alone at the threshing floor. Of course that is not so. This was a time of feasting and all of the household would camp around the threshing floor. There were many people present. After the feast and work was over for the day, the men would sleep around the grain pile, using it at a backrest with their feet sticking out from it like spokes on a wagon wheel. They slept this way to keep potential thieves from stealing their grain.

Ruth was to wait until Boaz had finished feasting and to

mark where he laid down at the grain pile to sleep. Then Ruth came quietly and laid down at his feet making her request of him to be her *goel*. At midnight, something startled Boaz out of his sleep and he discovers Ruth at his feet.

Boaz commends her for choosing him rather than one of the younger men and promises her he will do everything he can. He also informs her that a "nearer kinsman" than he existed. She remains at his feet until just before sunrise, whereby Boaz informs the rest of his servants to remain silent about Ruth's claim upon him.

Boaz fills her veil with as much barley as she can carry. She returns to the city of Bethlehem and Naomi. Naomi asks her (Ruth 3:16) if Boaz had accepted her request of redemption. At the end of Act III, Ruth informs Naomi of what Boaz instructed her to do. She is sitting waiting until he calls for her that same day as he promised (v. 18).

Act IV takes place at the city gates of Bethlehem. Boaz sees the nearer kinsman approaching and calls for him to come and do business. He then calls ten of the city elders to witness the transaction. Boaz lays out Naomi's desire to sell a parcel of ground to a "redeemer."

The "near kinsman" declares he will purchase the land. Then Boaz informs him that in the purchase of the land, he would also have the responsibility to Ruth, the wife of Mahlon, and to raise up a son to Mahlon's name. Upon this information, the nearer kinsman relinquishes his right of redemption to Boaz. The nearer kinsman publicly removed his shoe before the ten witnesses and gave it to Boaz, sealing the matter. This signified he gave up his right of redemption for that property forever to Boaz.

Boaz marries Ruth with the blessing of the people that were at the gate (4:11-12). Ruth bares a son, which the neighbors of Naomi name Obed, which means "worshipper."

Handfuls On Purpose
Studies in the Book of Ruth
Chapter One
Running Away From God

"¹ Now it came to pass in the days when the judges ruled, that there was a famine in the land. And a certain man of Bethlehemjudah went to sojourn in the country of Moab, he, and his wife, and his two sons. ² And the name of the man *was* Elimelech, and the name of his wife Naomi, and the name of his two sons Mahlon and Chilion, Ephrathites of Bethlehemjudah. And they came into the country of Moab, and continued there. ³ And Elimelech Naomi's husband died; and she was left, and her two sons. ⁴ And they took them wives of the women of Moab; the name of the one *was* Orpah, and the name of the other Ruth: and they dwelled there about ten years. ⁵ And Mahlon and Chilion died also both of them; and the woman was left of her two sons and her husband" (Ruth 1:1-5).

Ruth is a wonderful little book of four chapters detailing the life of a woman named Ruth. Although it records an accurate history of a period of about eleven years, it is also a book of types represented by the individual characters in the book.

The book of Ruth gives us the first hint of the Church Age in the Old Testament represented by Ruth, the Gentile bride of Boaz (who is a type of Christ, our Kinsman Redeemer). Naomi represents the nation of Israel under chastisement and later, restoration and blessing.

In Ruth 1:1, we see the historical setting to be "in the days when the Judges ruled" (or judged). The Midrash (Rabbinical commentaries) makes Ruth a daughter of the Moabite king Eglon who Ehud killed in the first 100 years of the period of the Judges. However, Josephus (the Jewish historian at the time of Christ) places Boaz as a contemporary with Eli, which would put the events of the book of Ruth at the end of the book of Judges. This is about three-hundred years after the entrance into the Promised Land under Joshua (this seems the most probable). This fact is important in order to understand the overall spiritual climate of the nation of Israel during this historical period.

First, in order to understand the purpose of the "famine in the land" of Ruth 1:1, we need to go back to Judges 2:11-18 to see the four-phase sin cycle of each succeeding generation of Israel.

> "[11] And the children of Israel did evil in the sight of the LORD, and served Baalim: [12] And they forsook the LORD God of their fathers, which brought them out of the land of Egypt, and followed other gods, of the gods of the people that *were* round about them, and bowed themselves unto them, and provoked the LORD to anger. [13] And they forsook the LORD, and served Baal and Ashtaroth. [14] And the anger of the LORD was hot against Israel, and he delivered them into the hands of spoilers that spoiled them, and he sold them into the hands of their enemies round about, so that they could not any longer stand before their enemies. [15] Whithersoever they went out, the hand of the LORD was against them for evil, as the LORD had said, and as the LORD had sworn unto them: and they were greatly distressed. [16] Nevertheless the LORD raised up judges, which delivered them out of the hand of those that spoiled them. [17] And yet they would not hearken unto their judges, but they went a whoring after other gods, and bowed themselves unto them: they turned quickly out of the way which their fathers walked in, obeying the commandments of the LORD; *but* they did not so. [18] And when the LORD raised them up judges, then the LORD was with the judge, and delivered them out of the hand of their enemies all the days of the judge: for it repented the LORD because of their groanings by reason of them that oppressed them and vexed them" (Judges 2:11-18).

First Phase of the Sin Cycle: Judges 2:11-13

This phase begins with apathy and complacency toward the things of God and His expectations of holiness and purity. It culminates with the intermixing of pagan worship and worldly practices with the things of God. Eventually this progression would end with "forsaking" or abandoning the Lord (v. 12). The people then accepted total paganism and worldliness as each generation allowed a little more of God's absolutes to slip through their fingers.

Second Phase of the Sin Cycle: Judges 2:14

Once they began to move away from purity and holiness (separation), God's chastisement would come upon them in the degree necessary to turn them back to Him and His truths (repentance). In Ruth, the chastisement is in the form of a famine that is a lesser degree of chastisement than a conquering and oppressive nation. The oppressive nation would attack, steal, destroy their possessions, ravage their wives and daughters, and enslave those left alive. In this second phase, God's hand of protection and blessing is withdrawn. It was God's intention to prove to His people that they could not survive without His help.

Third Phase of the Sin Cycle: Judges 2:18

Once the people were under chastisement and oppressed by their captors in slavery, they would begin to *remember* the God they professed to know and worship. They would begin to cry out to Him in prayerful repentance. God would hear their crying and groaning and have mercy on them.

Fourth Phase of the Sin Cycle: Judges 2:19

In this phase, God would raise up judges to deliver them out of bondage and lead them back to righteousness, holiness, and purity. According to Judges 2:19, this cycle repeats itself throughout the book of Judges and throughout the Old Testament. (It is also true of New Testament believers.)

> " And it came to pass, when the judge was dead, *that* they returned, and corrupted *themselves* more than their fathers, in following other gods to serve them, and to bow down unto them; they ceased not from their own doings, nor from their stubborn way" (Judges 2:19).

However, notice the progressive increase in wickedness with each repeat of the sin cycle. This tendency continues today. This is why pastors need to teach each succeeding generation the same historic truths of God and encourage obedience in keeping these historic truths. The tendency is to invite the world and its corruptions into the home and into the church. When that happens, the Christian (individually), and the Church (corporately), begins to lose their distinctiveness and their power with God - separation from the world is critical to power with God. This is why there is a constant battle for each new generation in the Church. When moms and dads begin to become *soft* on the things of God, they are sealing the fate of their children under God's chastisement.

The last verse of the book of Judges provides another important point to our understanding of the book of Ruth.

"In those days *there was* no king in Israel: every man did *that which was* right in his own eyes" (Judges 21:25).

Ruth 1:1-5 represents the consequences of Judges 21:25. The people of Israel were very much like Christians today. They wanted God's blessing and provision for them, but not His authority over them. They wanted God to be accountable to them, but they did not want to be accountable to Him. They wanted a distant God when it came to their unfaithful practices, but a near God when it came to their wants and needs. They wanted God to be a faithful husband to them, while they were an unfaithful wife to Him.

These things magnify the great contrast between Judges 21:25 and the name Elimelech of Ruth 1:1. Elimelech means *God is my King*. That was the testimony of Israel, but it was a lie. It was the farthest thing from the truth of their lives (the practice of their beliefs).

"[7] *Ye* hypocrites, well did Esaias prophesy of you, saying, [8] This people draweth nigh unto me with their mouth, and honoureth me with *their* lips; but their heart is far from me" (Matthew 15:7-8).

Just like the Christians of today who say *Jesus is Lord*, it did not mean anything to them. Like the pick-up truck in a parking lot one day - on one side of the bumper was a sticker saying *Jesus Is Lord*. On the same bumper on the other side was a sticker promoting abortion.

In Ruth 1:1, Israel is in the second phase of the sin cycle. Famine is in the land. God's chastisement is upon Israel to turn their hearts back to Him. Elimelech sees it as a small inconvenience and decides to "sojourn in the country of Moab." ("Sojourn" refers to a short visit.) The problem is that Elimelech was trying to escape the chastisement of God. That is not possible.

The word "Bethlehemjudah" means the *house of bread in the land of praise*. At this point in history, there was no bread in the *house of bread* because there was no genuine praise in the *land of praise*. Instead of stopping and evaluating the change that was needed (repentance), Elimelech takes his family, leaves the *house of bread* in the *land of praise,* and heads for Moab.

Moab was a wicked, Baalistic nation that descended from one of the two sons of the incestuous relationship of Lot with his two daughters (Benammi was the other son and was the father of the Ammonites). It is apparent that, although Lot got his two daughters out of Sodom, he never got Sodom out of his daughters. They transferred the wickedness of Sodom too their two sons. God would use Moab to turn the heart of Israel back to Him.

" Moab *is* my washpot *{lit., boiling caldron for cleansing}*; over Edom will I cast out my shoe; over Philistia will I triumph" (Psalm 108:9).

God would use Moab as a cleansing place, where God would bring Israel (typified by Naomi) face to face with the cause of her chastisement. God wanted Israel to change the *way* they lived. Instead, like a rebellious teen-ager, they ran away from home to avoid God's chastisement and only changed the *place* they lived. Changing the place they lived could not change their ways or restore them to the place of blessing and happiness. They needed a change of heart, not a change of place. We cannot proclaim God to be King (Lord) and at the same time be having a love affair with the world.

"[15] Love not the world, neither the things *that are* in the world. If any man love the world, the love of the Father is not in him. [16] For all that *is* in the world, the lust of the flesh, and the lust of the eyes, and the pride of life, is not of the Father, but is of the world. [17] And the world passeth away, and the lust thereof: but he that doeth the will of God abideth for ever" (I John 2:15-17).

When the happiness and joy of your Christianity is gone and chastisement is upon you, running from God is a dangerous thing to do. It was in running away from God's fixed place (where God had put them) that showed how unfaithful Israel was to their testimony (God is my King). God *spanked* them. Instead of repenting and seeking forgiveness and reconciliation, they ran away from home. Things do not change much, do they?

Handfuls On Purpose
Studies in the Book of Ruth
Chapter One
Running Away From God

1. Ruth is a historical book representing about an 11 year period of history during the period of the Judges. It also is a book of types.
   A. Of whom is Ruth typical?
   B. Of whom is Boaz typical?
   C. Of whom is Naomi typical?

2. Why is it important to understand the chronological period of the book of Ruth?

3. The reason behind the *famine in the land* of Ruth 1:1 is detailed in the four phase Sin Cycle of Judges 2:11-18. Detail these four phases.

   A. Phase One, Judges 2:11-13: How does this truth apply to your life?
   B. Phase Two, Judges 2:14: How does this truth apply to your life?
   C. Phase Three, Judges 2:18: How does this truth apply to your life?
   D. Phase Four, Judges 2:16: How does this truth apply to your life?

4. What does Judges 2:19 tell us about the repetition of this sin cycle in progressive generations?

5. What must we **do** for our children in order to help them avoid this sin cycle in their generation?

6. What must we **be** for our children in order to help them avoid this sin cycle in their generation?

7. What about Judges 21:25 is reflected by the consequences of Ruth 1:1-5?

8. What is the contrast of Judges 21:25 with the meaning of the name *Elimelech* in Ruth?

9. When Israel professed God to be their King, was that a truth manifested by the way they lived?

10. In what way is it similar today, when many Christians profess that Jesus is Lord?

11. What causes God to chastise His children? Is chastisement intended to punish them? What is the purpose of chastisement?

12. What does the word "sojourn" mean in Ruth 1:1?

13. What was Elimelech trying to do in response to God's chastisement by going to Moab?

14. What is a literal translation of the word "Bethlehemjudah"?

15. From whom did the nation of Moab descend and why were they so wicked?

16. From Psalm 108:9, what does the word "washpot" mean and how does that relate to what God would do with the family of Elimelech in Moab?

17. God wanted Israel to change the _____ they lived. Instead, they ran away from God's chastisement and only changed the _____ they lived.

18. We cannot proclaim God to be our King, and have a love _____ at the same time with the world.

19. How does I John 2:15 confirm the statement of your answer to the above question?

20. Do you think Christians ever *run away from home* when they come under chastisement?
    A. Do you think that this is a spiritually mature thing to do?
    B. Do you think that the person who would do so understands the principle of biblical discipline?

Handfuls On Purpose
Studies in the Book of Ruth
Chapter Two
Learning To Fear the Lord

"[1] Now it came to pass in the days when the judges ruled, that there was a famine in the land. And a certain man of Bethlehemjudah went to sojourn in the country of Moab, he, and his wife, and his two sons. [2] And the name of the man *was* Elimelech, and the name of his wife Naomi, and the name of his two sons Mahlon and Chilion, Ephrathites of Bethlehemjudah. And they came into the country of Moab, and continued there. [3] And Elimelech Naomi's husband died; and she was left, and her two sons. [4] And they took them wives of the women of Moab; the name of the one *was* Orpah, and the name of the other Ruth: and they dwelled there about ten years. [5] And Mahlon and Chilion died also both of them; and the woman was left of her two sons and her husband" (Ruth 1:1-5).

If we are going to understand that Naomi typifies Israel, we need to understand Ruth 1:1 as it refers to what was happening in Israel at the time when the Judges ruled. Josephus[3], the great Jewish historian at the time of Christ, places Boaz as a contemporary of Eli who judged Israel for forty years, from BC 1108 until BC 1068.

Before we look at Eli, who he was and what kind of man he was, we want to look at the military situation existing in Israel at the time of Ruth. Israel was in the second phase of the four-phase sin cycle of Judges 2:14.

" And the anger of the LORD was hot against Israel, and he delivered them into the hands of spoilers that spoiled them, and he sold them into the hands of their enemies round about, so that they could not any longer stand before their enemies" (Judges 2:14).

When the famine is removed from Israel, it is the fourth phase of the sin cycle as detailed in Judges 2:16.

"Nevertheless the LORD raised up judges, which delivered them out of the hand of those that spoiled them" (Judges 2:16).

---

[3] Josephus, Flavius. *Josephus Complete Works*. Translated by William Whiston. Grand Rapids: Kregel Publications, 1980.

According to Ruth 1:4, we know Naomi stayed in Moab about ten years or more. We also know from Old Testament chronology that if Eli was at Shiloh in BC 1108, he was there at the beginning of the eighteen year Ammonite oppression of Judges 10:6-8.

"⁶ And the children of Israel did evil again in the sight of the LORD, and served Baalim, and Ashtaroth, and the gods of Syria, and the gods of Zidon, and the gods of Moab, and the gods of the children of Ammon, and the gods of the Philistines, and forsook the LORD, and served not him. ⁷ And the anger of the LORD was hot against Israel, and he sold them into the hands of the Philistines, and into the hands of the children of Ammon. ⁸ And that year they vexed and oppressed the children of Israel: eighteen years, all the children of Israel that *were* on the other side Jordan in the land of the Amorites, which *is* in Gilead" (Judges 10:6-8).

This is probably the cause behind the famine in the land of Israel as recorded in the book of Ruth. By the time Naomi and Ruth returned to Bethlehem, it was probably at the end of the Ammonite oppression when Eli and Jephthah were Judges in Israel. Jephthah judged in Gilead on the East side of the Jordon in the Transjordan area. Eli judged on the West side of the Jordon at Shiloh as High Priest of Israel. So in Judges 10:6-8, we find the spiritual condition of Israel at the time of the book of Ruth. **I Samuel 2:12-17 and 22 tells us why this spiritual condition existed in Israel.**

"¹² Now the sons of Eli *were* sons of Belial; they knew not the LORD. ¹³ And the priests' custom with the people *was, that*, when any man offered sacrifice, the priest's servant came, while the flesh was in seething, with a fleshhook of three teeth in his hand; ¹⁴ And he struck *it* into the pan, or kettle, or caldron, or pot; all that the fleshhook brought up the priest took for himself. So they did in Shiloh unto all the Israelites that came thither. ¹⁵ Also before they burnt the fat, the priest's servant came, and said to the man that sacrificed, Give flesh to roast for the priest; for he will not have sodden flesh of thee, but raw. ¹⁶ And *if* any man said unto him, Let them not fail to burn the fat presently, and *then* take *as much* as thy soul desireth; then he would answer him, *Nay*; but thou shalt give *it me* now: and if not, I will take *it* by force. ¹⁷ Wherefore the sin of the young men was very great before the LORD: for men abhorred the offering of the LORD . . . ²² Now Eli was very old, and heard all that his sons did unto all Israel; and how they lay with the women that assembled {*lit. assembled by troops*} *at* the door of the tabernacle of the congregation" (I Samuel 2:12-17, 22).

Needless to say, the Tabernacle environment was very ungodly. Eli was the High Priest. We find some details about what kind of man Eli was in I Samuel 1:12-14.

"¹² And it came to pass, as she continued praying before the LORD, that Eli marked her mouth. ¹³ Now Hannah, she spake in her heart; only her lips moved, but her voice was not heard: therefore Eli thought she had been drunken. ¹⁴ And Eli said unto her, How long wilt thou be drunken? put away thy wine from thee" (I Samuel 1:12-14).

Hannah, a godly woman, replies to Eli's accusation against her.

"¹⁵ And Hannah answered and said, No, my lord, I *am* a woman of a sorrowful spirit: I have drunk neither wine nor strong drink, but have poured out my soul before the LORD. ¹⁶ Count not thine handmaid for a daughter of Belial: for out of the abundance of my complaint and grief have I spoken hitherto" (I Samuel 1:15-16).

Eli was accustomed to seeing drunken women in the Tabernacle and was apparently used to tolerating them. Why was Eli accustomed to seeing drunken women in the Tabernacle?

" Now Eli was very old, and heard all that his sons did unto all Israel; and how they lay with the women that assembled *at* the door of the tabernacle of the congregation" (I Samuel 2:22).

This was much more than sexual sin (as wicked as that was). In the religion of Baalism, the priests of Baal were also male prostitutes who had sexual relations with the women who came to the Temple of Baal to worship Baal. Hophni and Phinehas had actually incorporated Baalism into the Tabernacle worship of God. Jehovah was their God, but they adopted a form of Baal worship to worship Him. This was the military, spiritual, and religious atmosphere typified by Naomi in Moab. Is there any wonder why God's chastisement was upon Israel and why there was famine in the land?

All during this time, Israel is proclaiming God to be her King. What was the name of the husband of Naomi again? (Elimelech) What did it mean? Why did Eli not do something about his sons? He did not act because his role as the High Priest was the next thing to being a king in Israel (there was no king at this time). Eli's sons would inherit his position.

What was the reason the people of Israel did not do something about the wickedness? They did not act because most of them did not really care. Many of them enjoyed it. Others just said it was not their problem. We should never forget that in all periods of history (of Israel or the Church), God has placed the responsibility for purity upon those calling themselves His children.

"[1] It is reported commonly *that there is* fornication among you, and such fornication as is not so much as named among the Gentiles, that one should have his father's wife. [2] And ye are puffed up, and have not rather mourned, that he that hath done this deed might be taken away from among you. [3] For I verily, as absent in body, but present in spirit, have judged already, as though I were present, *concerning* him that hath so done this deed, [4] In the name of our Lord Jesus Christ, when ye are gathered together, and my spirit, with the power of our Lord Jesus Christ, [5] To deliver such an one unto Satan for the destruction of the flesh, that the spirit may be saved in the day of the Lord Jesus. [6] Your glorying *is* not good. Know ye not that a little leaven leaveneth the whole lump? [7] Purge out therefore the old leaven, that ye may be a new lump, as ye are unleavened. For even Christ our passover is sacrificed for us:" (I Corinthians 5:1-7).

Israel's leadership was not accountable to God because Israel was not accountable to God. Neither the people or the priests feared Him. God would use chastisement to teach them to fear Him.

" The fear of the LORD *is* the beginning {*lit, the principal part*} of knowledge: *but* fools despise wisdom and instruction" (Proverbs 1:7).

If a person can continue to live in the flesh without fearing God for the consequences, he needs to go back to *spiritual kindergarten*. Chastisement takes you there. How do you know if you are a Christian who lives in the flesh? You will know because you will manifest the "works of the flesh" through your life.

"[19] Now the works of the flesh are manifest, which are *these*; Adultery, fornication, uncleanness, lasciviousness, [20] Idolatry, witchcraft, hatred, variance, emulations, wrath, strife, seditions, heresies, [21] Envyings, murders, drunkenness, revellings, and such like: of the which I tell you before, as I have also told *you* in time past, that they which do such things shall not inherit the kingdom of God" (Galatians 5:19-21).

If any of the things listed in Galatians 5:19-21 are continually or habitually evident in your life, you need to be "born again" or you need to learn to fear the Lord. God will take you back to spiritual kindergarten with chastisement.

What was the first motivational truth every Jew was to teach His children?

"[1] Now these *are* the commandments, the statutes, and the judgments, which the LORD your God commanded to teach you, that ye might do *them* in the land whither ye go to possess it: [2] <u>That thou mightest fear the LORD thy God</u>, to keep all his statutes and his commandments, which I command thee, thou, and thy son, and thy son's son, all the days of thy life; and that thy days may be prolonged. [3] Hear therefore, O Israel, and observe to do *it*; that it may be well with thee, and that ye may increase mightily, as the LORD God of thy fathers hath promised thee, in the land that floweth with milk and honey" (Deuteronomy 6:1-3).

They were to teach their children to fear the Lord before they taught them to love the Lord (Deuteronomy 6:4-9). What does it mean to "fear the Lord"? It was an Old Testament phrase of piety. It combined a reverential trust of God with a hatred of evil (sin).

Have you taught your children to fear the Lord? Do you have a reverence of God and a hatred of any form of evil? If you do not, perhaps that is why your children do not fear the Lord.

Can you remember the last time one of your children saw something wrong on T.V. and you turned it off or changed the channel in the middle of a show? When was the last time you got angry over something you saw that was wrong? If righteous indignation does not boil in your soul because of the murder of thousands of babies each day, you do not fear the Lord! If you are not embroiled over young children being taught homosexuality as an *alternative lifestyle*, you do not fear the Lord! If lying is the normal thing you do if you want to be elected or get somewhere in this world, you do not fear the Lord!

Do you think Naomi learned to fear the Lord after what happened to her in Moab? What would you think of someone who had to repeat kindergarten repeatedly? Chastisement always takes us back to *spiritual kindergarten*. Many Christians have had to repeat kindergarten often. Many of us will be back there repeatedly until we finally learn to fear the Lord.

If you have not learned to fear the Lord (reverence Him and hate sin), you do not know the God of the Bible the way He wants you to know Him. Why did Israel (and Christians today) not fear the Lord? God was not *real* to them. How do we know that?

"^{1} And the word of Samuel came to all Israel. Now Israel went out against the Philistines to battle, and pitched beside Ebenezer: and the Philistines pitched in Aphek. ^{2} And the Philistines put themselves in array against Israel: and when they joined battle, Israel was smitten before the Philistines: and they slew of the army in the field about four thousand men. ^{3} And when the people were come into the camp, the elders of Israel said, Wherefore hath the LORD smitten us to day before the Philistines? Let us fetch the ark of the covenant of the LORD out of Shiloh unto us, that, when it cometh among us, it may save us out of the hand of our enemies" (I Samuel 4:1-3).

Israel had reduced the Ark of the Covenant to an idol. God was not real to them. If you do not fear the Lord, He probably is not real to you either. If you want to learn to fear the Lord, God has to become real to you. Learning to fear the Lord comes from an accurate knowledge of who and what He is. Yes, He is a God of love, but He is also a God who hates sin.

"^{16} These six *things* doth the LORD hate: yea, seven *are* an abomination unto him: ^{17} A proud look, a lying tongue, and hands that shed innocent blood, ^{18} An heart that deviseth wicked imaginations, feet that be swift in running to mischief, ^{19} A false witness *that* speaketh lies, and he that soweth discord among brethren" (Proverbs 6:16-19).

Something that is an "abomination" is something that is

detestable and disgusting to you. To learn to fear God means to learn to have the same attitudes towards sin that He does, even the sin in your own life. When you have that attitude towards all sin, it will produce genuine repentance in your life.

Christianity is so much more than a bunch of rules and regulations. Christianity is defined as a personal relationship between a person and the living God who is the Creator of Heaven, earth, and all that is in them. That God loves you. All He asks of you is to love Him in return. To love Him means to trust Him reverentially as the one who created you and who knows what is best for your life.

Can you reverentially trust Him? Can you accept the fact that if God hates something, it is best if you learn to hate it too? To fear the Lord is a decision of the heart. Will you decide to fear the Lord today?

Handfuls On Purpose
Studies in the Book of Ruth
Chapter Two
Learning To Fear the Lord

1. Of whom does Josephus (the Jewish historian at the time of Christ) tell us Boaz was a contemporary?

2. When did Eli judge Israel? BC 110_____ BC 106_____

3. Read Judges 2:14 and Ruth 1:1-5 together. What phase of the four-phase sin cycle was Israel in at this time?

4. Read Judges 2:16 and Ruth 1:6 together. What phase of the four-phase sin cycle was Israel in at this time?

5. Read Ruth 1:4. How long did Naomi stay in Moab?

6. Read Judges 10:6-8. What was happening in Israel that began in BC 1106?

7. From Judges 10:6-8 we can discover the conditions existing in Israel at the time of the book of Ruth. Read I Samuel 2:12-17. What was the spiritual condition behind all of this?

8. Read I Samuel 1:12-14. What do these verses reveal to us about Eli's character (compare 2:12 and 22)?

9. According to I Samuel 2:22, what had Hophni and Phinehas actually incorporated into the Tabernacle worship of Jehovah?

10. Why did Eli not do something about his sons? What was he trying to protect for future generations of his family?

11. Why did the people of Israel not rise up and do something about this wickedness at the Tabernacle of God?

12. Read I Corinthians 5:1-7. Upon whom has God placed the responsibility for a pure Church?
    A. Does that mean the Church should be involved in a *witch-hunt* mentality?
    B. When unrepentant people refuse to do what is right, who does God hold responsible to deal with them?

14. Why was Israel's leadership not held accountable to God by God's people?

15. Read Proverbs 1:7. What was the *kindergarten truth* Israel had not yet learned?

16. Read Galatians 5:19-21. What reveals a person who does not know enough to fear the Lord? How would that person recognize himself as someone who does not fear the Lord?

17. If you have not learned to fear the Lord, what will God have to do to teach you to do so?

18. From Deuteronomy 6:1-3, what was the first motivational truth every Jew was to teach his children?

19. Define what it means to fear the Lord. The fear of the Lord is a reverential _____ of God accompanied by a _____ of evil.

    A. Do you suppose God might begin to measure the success of parenthood by this standard?
    B. Based upon the above definition of the fear of the Lord, do you think you have taught your children to fear Him?
    C. Based upon the above definition, can you honestly say you fear Him?
    D. If you as a parent do not fear the Lord, do you think you will be able to teach your children to fear Him?
    E. If this is all true, does your success as a parent and the success of succeeding generations of Christians depend upon you learning to fear the Lord?

20. Define *righteous indignation* and how it relates to the manifestation of the fear of the Lord in a life.

21. From the foundation we have laid thus far, how important to the Lord is our learning to fear the Lord?

22. Read 1 Samuel 4:1-3. What was Israel's attitude toward the Ark of the Covenant that reveals that God was not real to them?
    A. Is God real to you?
    B. How do you know if He is real to you?

23. Read Proverbs 6:16-19. What are some of the *things* that God *hates?*

24. If you fear the Lord, will you have learned to hate these things too?

25. Define *ABOMINATION.*
    A. Is that your attitude toward the things of Proverbs 6:16-19?
    B. If not, do you fear the Lord?

Handfuls On Purpose
Studies in the Book of Ruth
Chapter Three
Removing the Blinders of Time to See the Blessings of Eternity

"^{6} Then she arose with her daughters in law, that she might return from the country of Moab: for she had heard in the country of Moab how that the LORD had visited his people in giving them bread. ^{7} Wherefore she went forth out of the place where she was, and her two daughters in law with her; and they went on the way to return unto the land of Judah. ^{8} And Naomi said unto her two daughters in law, Go, return each to her mother's house: the LORD deal kindly with you, as ye have dealt with the dead, and with me. ^{9} The LORD grant you that ye may find rest, each *of you* in the house of her husband. Then she kissed them; and they lifted up their voice, and wept" (Ruth 1:6-9).

Most people live and think in a temporal way. We often lock our plans for the future into temporal thinking. The whole book of Ecclesiastes reveals we are "under the sun" (this life only) thinkers. We are blind to the reality of another existence beyond the existence known by human senses.

"^{9} But as it is written, Eye hath not seen, nor ear heard, neither have entered into the heart of man, the things which God hath prepared for them that love him. ^{10} But God hath revealed *them* unto us by his Spirit: for the Spirit searcheth all things, yea, the deep things of God. ^{11} For what man knoweth the things of a man, save the spirit of man which is in him? even so the things of God knoweth no man, but the Spirit of God. ^{12} Now we have received, not the spirit of the world, but the spirit which is of God; that we might know the things that are freely given to us of God" (I Corinthians 2:9-12).

In Ruth 1:7, Naomi is ready to leave Moab (God's boiling cauldron for cleansing, Psalm 108:9). She went to Moab with her husband (Elimelech) because there was famine in the land of Judah due to God's chastisement. In Moab, the family of Naomi tried to escape that chastisement. In reality, they were running away from God's appointed place for them (Bethlehem). They ran away from home like rebellious teenagers not wanting to live under dad's and mom's rules. God wanted them to change the *way* they live.

Instead, they only changed the *place* they lived. While at Moab, they would learn to fear the Lord. To fear the Lord is a reverential trust of God accompanied by a hatred for evil.

To review the types, Naomi represents Israel under chastisement and restoration. The name Elimelech means *God is my king* and represents the destroyed testimony of Israel due to her spiritual unfaithfulness in idolatry and disobedience. In Ruth 1:3, Elimelech dies. Mahlon and Chilion represent the next generation of the children of Israel and the effect the unfaithfulness and idolatry the preceding generation had upon them. Their names mean *sickness* and *consumption*. The same principles continue through all generations, even to today. In Ruth 1:4, that generation dies in Moab.

Naomi (Israel) is alone in the middle of a Gentile nation in an unscriptural unity of illegitimate marriages to Gentile women. Israel had lost her distinctiveness as a people of God due to her failure to live according to the statutes and commandments of God. In Ruth 1:6, we find the story expanding beyond the failure in Moab to God's restoration in Bethlehem. This is the fourth phase of the sin cycle. Israel under chastisement cries out to God for deliverance. God answers. The famine is over.

Once again, there is bread in the House of Bread (Bethlehem; Ruth 1:6). This may typify the coming of Messiah. It is certainly true that God's intention in redemption is to redeem both Jew and Gentile alike.

> " For I am not ashamed of the gospel of Christ: for it is the power of God unto salvation to every one that believeth; to the Jew first, and also to the Greek {*or Gentile*}" (Romans 1:16).

> "[12] For there is no difference between the Jew and the Greek: for the same Lord over all is rich unto all that call upon him. [13] For whosoever shall call upon the name of the Lord shall be saved" (Romans 10:12-13).

In Ruth 1:7, we find a Jewish woman joined together with two Gentile women because of the marriage compromise of her two sons. These three women begin to head to the House of Bread (Bethlehem) in the Land of Praise (Judah) because the "Lord had visited His people" in giving them bread. This is another reason this may typify the coming of Messiah.

"³² Then Jesus said unto them, Verily, verily, I say unto you, Moses gave you not that bread from heaven; but my Father giveth you the true bread from heaven. ³³ For the bread of God is he which cometh down from heaven, and giveth life unto the world. ³⁴ Then said they unto him, Lord, evermore give us this bread. ³⁵ And Jesus said unto them, I am the bread of life: he that cometh to me shall never hunger; and he that believeth on me shall never thirst. ³⁶ But I said unto you, That ye also have seen me, and believe not. ³⁷ All that the Father giveth me shall come to me; and him that cometh to me I will in no wise cast out. ³⁸ For I came down from heaven, not to do mine own will, but the will of him that sent me. ³⁹ And this is the Father's will which hath sent me, that of all which he hath given me I should lose nothing, but should raise it up again at the last day. ⁴⁰ And this is the will of him that sent me, that every one which seeth the Son, and believeth on him, may have everlasting life: and I will raise him up at the last day. ⁴¹ The Jews then murmured at him, because he said, I am the bread which came down from heaven" (John 6:32-41).

On the journey (Ruth 1:8) to the Land of Praise, Naomi begins to tell her Gentile daughter-in-laws what they will have to give up if they go with her. Naomi knew what awaited her at Bethlehem - poverty, servitude, and difficulty. In this time of great difficulty, Naomi seems completely ignorant of God's intent to restore her and His overwhelming love for her. God's hand of correction had touched her life.

In such moments, people do not see the love and grace of God behind it all. She filled her thinking with discouragement, hopelessness, and despair. She saw herself in a hopeless situation (Ruth 1:12). It is from this perspective she speaks to her two daughter-in-laws (Ruth 1:12-13).

When Naomi says, "For it grieveth me," she reveals that she is filled with bitterness because of the "hand of the LORD" (referring to her chastisement). Naomi is still seeing her situation from a *temporal* perspective of life. She just cannot seem to see beyond her own circumstances to see God's eternal working in her life. As a result, each misfortune of her life increases her bitterness toward God and the hopelessness of her situation. Like many people, Naomi is making decisions in life based upon a fatalistic view of God's workings.

These kinds of difficulties often rise like a mountain range on the horizon, blocking our view of God's eternal workings. Paul (the Apostle of hope) helps every Christian to look beyond the inconveniences of this life to beyond the mountain ranges of pain and suffering into the eternity. We must learn to keep our vision fixed upon the eternal.

> " If in this life only { *'under the Sun'*} we have hope in Christ, we are of all men most miserable" (I Corinthians 15:19).

You only have one life to live. Live it to the fullest. This seems to be Naomi's philosophy of life. Solomon possessed this same "under the sun" perspective for the majority of his life.

> "[1] The words of the Preacher, the son of David, king in Jerusalem. [2] Vanity of vanities, saith the Preacher, vanity of vanities; all *is* vanity. [3] What profit hath a man of all his labour which he taketh under the sun? [4] *One* generation passeth away, and *another* generation cometh: but the earth abideth for ever" (Ecclesiastes 1:1-4).

In Ecclesiastes 1:1-4, God reveals to us a man locked into a box called time. Solomon cannot seem to see out of it. The result of this restricted vision is a life of selfish pursuits ending in cynicism, bitterness, and self-pity. God gives him a glimpse into eternity, but he just cannot seem to see beyond the walls of the box into which he has put himself.

For the Christian the answer is simple. **It is the Book. It is the Book.** Learn to look at life through the eternal truths of the Word of God. Until we learn to do so, we (like Solomon and Naomi) will continue to make bad decisions based upon what we see with our physical eyes. We will not see the spiritual reality available only to those with eyes of faith.

> "[12] I the Preacher was king over Israel in Jerusalem. [13] And I gave my heart to seek and search out by wisdom concerning all *things* that are done under heaven: this sore travail hath God given to the sons of man to be exercised {or, to afflict them} therewith. [14] I have seen all the works that are done under the sun; and, behold, all *is* vanity and vexation of spirit. [15] *That which is* crooked cannot be made straight: and that which is wanting cannot be numbered. [16] I communed with mine own heart, saying, Lo, I am come to great estate, and have gotten more wisdom than all *they* that have been before me in Jerusalem: yea, my heart had great experience of

wisdom and knowledge. ¹⁷ And I gave my heart to know wisdom, and to know madness and folly: I perceived that this also is vexation of spirit. ¹⁸ For in much wisdom *is* much grief: and he that increaseth knowledge increaseth sorrow" (Ecclesiastes 1:12-18).

However, even though it took a lifetime, Solomon got a new perspective on life.

" I know that, whatsoever God doeth, it shall be for ever: nothing can be put to it, nor any thing taken from it: and God doeth *it*, that *men* should fear before him" (Ecclesiastes 3:14).

"¹³ Let us hear the conclusion of the whole matter: Fear God, and keep his commandments: for this *is* the whole *duty* of man. ¹⁴ For God shall bring every work into judgment, with every secret thing, whether *it be* good, or whether *it be* evil" (Ecclesiastes 12:13-14).

All human beings are eternal. We will spend eternity somewhere. When we get our vision locked into a *temporal* ("under the Sun") perspective, we will begin to define God by what happens to us in this life. We even begin to define ourselves by what happens to us in this life. The spiritual reality is that God completely transcends this world and all that is in it (along with our souls). Satan does not want our vision of life to escape this world to see beyond this life into eternity.

"³ But if our gospel be hid, it is hid to them that are lost: ⁴ In whom the god of this world hath blinded the minds of them which believe not, lest the light of the glorious gospel of Christ, who is the image of God, should shine unto them" (II Corinthians 4:3-4).

Your life is but a small parenthesis in a short sentence in a never-ending volume of a novel called eternity. When we cannot (or when we refuse to) look beyond the parenthesis of our life to see the whole of which we are part, Satan will defeat us. When we do not keep our vision focused on God and eternity, we will end up wallowing in bitterness and self-pity just like Naomi. We will end up giving the kind of counsel that Naomi gave to Orpah and Ruth. From bad testimonies, there will always be the Orpahs who will abandon Christ and the difficulties of the Christian life to return to the world of comfort and convenience (which were really her old gods, 1:15).

Christ never said the Christian life would be easy. In fact, He said it would be just the opposite. The Christian must learn to cultivate a perspective of life that transcends this life and this world.

> "[13] Enter ye in at the strait gate: for wide *is* the gate, and broad *is* the way, that leadeth to destruction, and many there be which go in thereat [14] Because strait *is* the gate, and narrow {*literally: hard*} *is* the way, which leadeth unto life, and few there be that find it" (Matthew 7:13-14).

The Christian must learn to make choices and decisions in this life based upon a foundation of truth that transcends this life. Every decision and choice we make in this life affects eternity. Not just for ourselves, but also thousands of others living now and in the future. This is not about *pie in the sky*. We need to understand we are already living in our eternity. Just as the choice you made to get an education determined the job you presently have and the life you provide for yourself and your family, the elementary decisions we make every day in our present life will determine the eternal destiny of hundreds (perhaps thousands) of people, including yourself.

The first and foremost question of life is simple. What have you decided to do about Christ and your need of salvation? Are you saved and sure of it? If not, when you finally step outside of your box called time (by death) and see your eternity for the first time, you are going to be in for quite a shock. That eternity will never change from that point forward.

The second question is, "If you are saved ("born again"), what have you decided to do with your new life in Christ?" The decisions you make are eternally important. You have just one life to live. You can invest it in this doomed world, or you can invest it into eternity by investing your life in truth. You can invest it into eternity by living that truth and by sharing the Gospel with others. Then, when you step out of this box called time into your eternity, you will find familiar faces of friends and family. That eternity will never change.

Those decisions are up to you. Is your Christianity real enough to invest the only lifetime you have left into eternity? The time to decide that is *now*!

Handfuls On Purpose
Studies in the Book of Ruth
Chapter Three
Removing the Blinders of Time to See the Blessings of Eternity

1. From Ruth 1:7, what was "the place where she was" and why was she there?

Some Questions for Review

2. What was Naomi's husband's name and what does it mean?

3. While under chastisement in Moab, what was God teaching Israel?

4. What does Naomi typify in the narrative of the book of Ruth?

5. What does Elimelech typify?

6. What do Mahlon and Chilion represent?

7. What two verses from the book of Romans show us God's desire to redeem both Jew and Gentile equally?
    A. Romans 1: _____
    B. Romans 10: _____

8. From Ruth 1:7-8, where specifically does this all take place? Is it in Moab, in between Moab and Judah, or at Bethlehem?

9. What kind of life did Naomi expect to have, once she returned to Bethlehemjudah?

10. From Ruth 1:12 and 13, what was Naomi lacking at this point in her life, which is the direct cause of her counsel to Orpah and Ruth?

11. What is her perspective on life and eternity from which her counsel flows?

12. What was the result of Naomi's perspective on her attitude toward God and toward life in general?
    A. Has that ever been in your perspective on life and caused you to have similar attitudes toward God and your life in general?
    B. Do you think that perspective allowed you to be fair toward God and toward life?

13. Paul was an Apostle of many things. Paul certainly was the Apostle of _____.

14. What does Paul mean in I Corinthians 15:19 by "If in this life only we have hope in Christ"? To what point in this life must we constantly be looking beyond in order to maintain a healthy eternal perspective?

15. According to Ecclesiastes 1:1-3, what is an "under the Sun" perspective of life?
    A. What was the *box* into which Solomon's mind was locked that blocked his vision of eternity?
    B. How do faith and trust in God help us escape that box in our present life? How do faith and trust change our perspective?
    C. How should that change in perspective change our decision making process?

16. When we are locked into a *temporal* ("under the sun") mentality, how does that affect the way we define God?
    A. From that same perspective, how do we begin to define ourselves and our self-worth?
    B. B Do you think that perspective can give an accurate definition of God or ourselves?
    C. If not, how important is it to change that perspective in our lives?

17. What does Satan want to keep your vision (perspective) fixed upon?
    A. What does Satan want to keep your vision (perspective) away from?

B. How must we learn to *see* in order to broaden the horizons of our vision beyond the temporal things of this life?

18. At this point in Naomi's life, was she wallowing in bitterness and self-pity?
    A. How does this affect her counsel to Orpah and Ruth?
    B. Do you think your life may be having the same affect on others that Naomi's life had on the eternal decision of Orpah?

19. The Christian must learn to cultivate a perspective that _____ this life and this world. The Christian must learn to make choices and decisions in this world based upon a foundation of truth that _____ this life and this world.

20. When does a person begin his eternity?
    A. What do you expect to discover, once you step out of this *box* called time into your eternity?
    B. How will your present day decisions about life and priorities affect what will await you in your eternity?

Handfuls On Purpose
Studies in the Book of Ruth
Chapter Four
Six Resolutions of Spiritual Commitment to Sanctification

"[10] And they said unto her, Surely we will return with thee unto thy people. [11] And Naomi said, Turn again, my daughters: why will ye go with me? *are* there yet *any more* sons in my womb, that they may be your husbands? [12] Turn again, my daughters, go *your way*; for I am too old to have an husband. If I should say, I have hope, *if* I should have an husband also to night, and should also bear sons; [13] Would ye tarry for them till they were grown? would ye stay for them from having husbands? nay, my daughters; for it grieveth me much {Heb.: I have much bitterness} for your sakes that the hand of the LORD is gone out against me. [14] And they lifted up their voice, and wept again: and Orpah kissed her mother in law; but Ruth clave unto her. [15] And she said, Behold, thy sister in law is gone back unto her people, and unto her gods: return thou after thy sister in law. [16] And Ruth said, Intreat me not to leave thee, *or* to return from following after thee: for whither thou goest, I will go; and where thou lodgest, I will lodge: thy people *shall be* my people, and thy God my God: [17] Where thou diest, will I die, and there will I be buried: the LORD do so to me, and more also, *if ought* but death part thee and me" (Ruth 1:10-17).

THE BAPTISM OF RUTH

If we were to ask what the greatest catastrophe of the twentieth century was, we would get many different answers. Some would say the first or second World War. Others might say the Jewish holocaust of Nazi Germany. Some might remember some devastating natural disaster or even the Muslim terrorist attack on the Twin Towers. Political conservatives might say the rapid advancement of liberalism, secular humanism, and socialism in our society.

From a Bible perspective, the greatest tragedy of the Twentieth Century is millions of Christians living in the greatest country in the world, enjoying the freedom and prosperity to share their faith in Christ and His Gospel with anyone and everyone, but who lack the commitment to do so.

There are too many people, who profess to be Christians, who are like Orpah in Ruth 1:14. They have affection for Christ, but no commitment to serve Him. They say they love Him, but at the first hint of difficulty, they leave Him to live according to the desires of their hearts.

This chapter will focus on these kinds of personal failures of individual Christians. We can view the confrontation of our commitment to Christ (or lack thereof) negatively or positively. It is always a positive action to evaluate our failures if we do so with the intent to change the way we live. We change the way we live in order to become more effective as Christians. Therefore, the focus of this chapter will be on what we can do to become the kind of Christian that God can use and bless. In most cases, this begins with a willingness to recognize certain things about our life and the willingness to commit to doing whatever is necessary to make the appropriate changes.

We can learn a great deal from Ruth's decision as revealed in Ruth 1:14-17. The decision reveals an understanding of the difficulties that would become part of her life if she went with Naomi and a commitment to go regardless of what her decision would cost her personally. Ruth's statement to Naomi reveals the character of a true disciple. This is the kind of commitment Christ expects of all true disciples.

> "^{25} And there went great multitudes with him: and he turned, and said unto them, ^{26} If any *man* come to me, and hate not his father, and mother, and wife, and children, and brethren, and sisters, yea, and his own life also, he cannot be my disciple. ^{27} And whosoever doth not bear his cross, and come after me, cannot be my disciple" (Luke 14:25-27).

"Ruth clave unto her" (Ruth 1:14).

The word "clave" renders the idea of individuals uniting or *being stuck together*. Ruth made herself inseparable from Naomi. That is what every Christian ought to do with Christ. Christians love to quote the verse where Christ says, "I will never leave thee, nor forsake thee" (Hebrews 13:5). This is Christ's promise of commitment to His relationship with us. Have we made a similar promise of commitment to our relationship with Him?

Ruth makes six resolutions of commitment to her relationship with Naomi (Ruth 1:16-17). These parallel the kind of commitment that should accompany water baptism for believers.

First - "Whither thou goest I will go." This is a commitment to follow. To most Christians this means a commitment to follow Christ anywhere . . . EXCEPT. . . anywhere where they might feel challenged or uncomfortable. This means anywhere except where someone might ask them to do something they might not want to do. This means anywhere except where it might cost them more than they are willing to pay. That is not the kind of commitment Christ expected of His followers.

> "[19] And a certain scribe came, and said unto him, Master, I will follow thee whithersoever thou goest. [20] And Jesus saith unto him, The foxes have holes, and the birds of the air *have* nests; but the Son of man hath not where to lay *his* head. [21] And another of his disciples said unto him, Lord, suffer me first to go and bury my father. [22] But Jesus said unto him, Follow me; and let the dead bury their dead. [23] And when he was entered into a ship, his disciples followed him. [24] And, behold, there arose a great tempest in the sea, insomuch that the ship was covered with the waves: but he was asleep. [25] And his disciples came to *him*, and awoke him, saying, Lord, save us: we perish. [26] And he saith unto them, Why are ye fearful, O ye of little faith? Then he arose, and rebuked the winds and the sea; and there was a great calm. [27] But the men marvelled, saying, What manner of man is this, that even the winds and the sea obey him" (Matthew 8:19-27)!

Discipleship (following Christ) is a commitment of faith that gives without any qualifications or restrictions upon it. When Ruth committed herself to follow Naomi to Bethlehemjudah, she knew it was not going to be easy. A life of faith does not necessarily know what tomorrow will bring, nor does it worry about it. A commitment to follow Christ is a willingness that is prepared to drink of His cup of death. Today, few Christians are willing to live for Christ, let alone die for Him.

Second - "Where thou lodgest, I will lodge." This is a commitment to fellowship. The commitment to fellowship is a commitment to walk with Christ. The commitment to fellowship is a commitment to live in holiness and to walk in truth.

> "³ That which we have seen and heard declare we unto you, that ye also may have fellowship with us: and truly our fellowship *is* with the Father, and with his Son Jesus Christ. ⁴ And these things write we unto you, that your joy may be full. ⁵ This then is the message which we have heard of him, and declare unto you, that God is light, and in him is no darkness at all. ⁶ If we say that we have fellowship with him, and walk in darkness, we lie, and do not the truth: ⁷ But if we walk in the light, as he is in the light, we have fellowship one with another, and the blood of Jesus Christ his Son cleanseth us from all sin" (I John 1:3-7).

Fellowship is an intimacy with Christ that involves a communion in "light" (truth). Fellowship is a partnership involving the mutual sharing of all the assets (personal abilities and material possessions) of the individuals involved.

> "³² And the multitude of them that believed were of one heart and of one soul: neither said any *of them* that ought of the things which he possessed was his own; but they had all things common. ³³ And with great power gave the apostles witness of the resurrection of the Lord Jesus: and great grace was upon them all. ³⁴ Neither was there any among them that lacked: for as many as were possessors of lands or houses sold them, and brought the prices of the things that were sold, ³⁵ And laid *them* down at the apostles' feet: and distribution was made unto every man according as he had need" (Acts 4:32-35).

Central to the commitment to fellowship with Christ is the commitment to abandon a life of sin and to walk and live in the truth of God's Word.

Third – "Thy people shall be my people." This is the commitment to identify one's self with the children of God. Ruth had to forsake her country (Moab) and her people's religious practices and culture (idolatry). Many people reject the Gospel of Jesus Christ because they know that doing so will require they change their religious practices and even the churches they attend. Others refuse to accept Christ because of what family members or friends will think of them.

Every Christian needs to remember that once he is "born again" of the Spirit of God, God removes him from the family of

Adam and places him as an adult child in the family of God. That means we have a responsibility to treat other Christians as brothers and sisters in Christ. The commitment to family is the commitment to love one another.

> "^{10} In this the children of God are manifest, and the children of the devil: whosoever doeth not righteousness is not of God, neither he that loveth not his brother. ^{11} For this is the message {*commandment*} that ye heard from the beginning, that we should love one another. ^{12} Not as Cain, *who* was of that wicked one, and slew his brother. And wherefore slew he him? Because his own works were evil, and his brother's righteous. ^{13} Marvel not, my brethren, if the world hate you. ^{14} We know that we have passed from death unto life, because we love the brethren. He that loveth not *his* brother abideth in death. ^{15} Whosoever hateth his brother is a murderer: and ye know that no murderer hath eternal life abiding in him. ^{16} Hereby perceive we the love *of God*, because he laid down his life for us: and we ought to lay down *our* lives for the brethren. ^{17} But whoso hath this world's good, and seeth his brother have need, and shutteth up his bowels *of compassion* from him, how dwelleth the love of God in him? ^{18} My little children, let us not love in word, neither in tongue; but in deed and in truth. ^{19} And hereby we know that we are of the truth, and shall assure our hearts before him" (I John 3:10-19).

The commitment to family is the commitment to unity in truth.

> "^{4} I rejoiced greatly that I found of thy children walking in truth, as we have received a commandment from the Father. ^{5} And now I beseech thee, lady, not as though I wrote a new commandment unto thee, but that which we had from the beginning, that we love one another. ^{6} And this is love, that we walk after his commandments. This is the commandment, That, as ye have heard from the beginning, ye should walk in it" (II John 1:4-6).

> "^{3} For I rejoiced greatly, when the brethren came and testified of the truth that is in thee, even as thou walkest in the truth. ^{4} I have no greater joy than to hear that my children walk in truth" (III John 1:3-4).

Fourth - "Thy God shall be my God." This is a commitment to the Lordship of Christ. The commitment to the Lordship of Christ recognizes two things:

1. His absolute authority over our life
2. Our accountability to that authority

"² Hear, O heavens, and give ear, O earth: for the LORD hath spoken, I have nourished and brought up children, and they have rebelled against me. ³ The ox knoweth his owner, and the ass his master's crib: *but* Israel doth not know, my people doth not consider. ⁴ Ah sinful nation, a people laden with iniquity, a seed of evildoers, children that are corrupters: they have forsaken the LORD, they have provoked the Holy One of Israel unto anger, they are gone away backward" (Isaiah 1:2-4).

These verses describe many modern day Christians. To them, God is a heavenly, white haired, old *Santa Claus* type who they try to manipulate into getting what they want when they want it. (Did you know that shopping centers are getting letters for Santa with death threats from kids if he does not give them what they want?) Commitment to the Lordship of Christ is a commitment to obey the Word of God.

"⁴³ For a good tree bringeth not forth corrupt fruit; neither doth a corrupt tree bring forth good fruit. ⁴⁴ For every tree is known by his own fruit. For of thorns men do not gather figs, nor of a bramble bush gather they grapes. ⁴⁵ A good man out of the good treasure of his heart bringeth forth that which is good; and an evil man out of the evil treasure of his heart bringeth forth that which is evil: for of the abundance of the heart his mouth speaketh. ⁴⁶ And why call ye me, Lord, Lord, and do not the things which I say? ⁴⁷ Whosoever cometh to me, and heareth my sayings, and doeth them, I will shew you to whom he is like: ⁴⁸ He is like a man which built an house, and digged deep, and laid the foundation on a rock: and when the flood arose, the stream beat vehemently upon that house, and could not shake it: for it was founded upon a rock. ⁴⁹ But he that heareth, and doeth not, is like a man that without a foundation built an house upon the earth; against which the stream did beat vehemently, and immediately it fell; and the ruin of that house was great" (Luke 6:43-49).

"³¹ Then said Jesus to those Jews which believed on him, If ye continue in my word, *then* are ye my disciples indeed; ³² And ye shall know the truth, and the truth shall make you free. ³³ They answered him, We be Abraham's seed, and were never in bondage to any man: how sayest thou, Ye shall be made free? ³⁴ Jesus answered them, Verily, verily, I say unto you, Whosoever committeth sin is the servant of sin. ³⁵ And the servant abideth not in the house for ever: *but* the Son abideth ever. ³⁶ If the Son therefore shall make you free, ye shall be free indeed. ³⁷ I know that ye are Abraham's seed; but ye seek to kill me, because my word hath no place in you" (John 8:31-37).

Fifth - "Where thou diest, I will die." This is the commitment to the sacrifice of self. This commitment defines the degree of our love for God and reveals a true comprehension of eternal realities. This kind of commitment was the common, normal, and expected level of commitment amongst early Christianity.

"⁵¹ Ye stiffnecked and uncircumcised in heart and ears, ye do always resist the Holy Ghost: as your fathers *did*, so *do* ye. ⁵² Which of the prophets have not your fathers persecuted? and they have slain them which shewed before of the coming of the Just One; of whom ye have been now the betrayers and murderers: ⁵³ Who have received the law by the disposition of angels, and have not kept *it*. ⁵⁴ When they heard these things, they were cut to the heart, and they gnashed on him with *their* teeth. ⁵⁵ But he {*Stephen*}, being full of the Holy Ghost, looked up stedfastly into heaven, and saw the glory of God, and Jesus standing on the right hand of God, ⁵⁶ And said, Behold, I see the heavens opened, and the Son of man standing on the right hand of God. ⁵⁷ Then they cried out with a loud voice, and stopped their ears, and ran upon him with one accord, ⁵⁸ And cast *him* out of the city, and stoned *him*: and the witnesses laid down their clothes at a young man's feet, whose name was Saul. ⁵⁹ And they stoned Stephen, calling upon *God*, and saying, Lord Jesus, receive my spirit. ⁶⁰ And he kneeled down, and cried with a loud voice, Lord, lay not this sin to their charge. And when he had said this, he fell asleep" (Acts 7:51-60).

Stephen understood the danger when he preached this message to the lost Jews. Yet he preached what God wanted him to say and willingly died for it. Most people today consider this kind of commitment fanaticism. It is a willingness to say, be, or do whatever is required of the moment and circumstance regardless of the cost to us personally. In our present twentieth century society, it is socially and culturally acceptable to be a fanatic about anything but *religion*. A person can be a fanatic about sports, work, and even politics. You cross the line when you become an extremist about religion. There are people who could quote you the batting averages of every player on their favorite baseball team (and would not hesitate to do so if you let them). Yet, if you memorize a few verses of Scripture, you are a religious nut.

Sixth - "If ought but death part thee and me." This is the commitment to the long haul (service or work). Christian service is what the Bible calls "the <u>work</u> of the ministry." We should not give anything in this life priority over the "work of the ministry." We cannot define faithfulness to Christ apart from being faithful in DOING the "work of the ministry."

> "[11] And he gave some, apostles; and some, prophets; and some, evangelists; and some, pastors and teachers; [12] For the perfecting of the saints, for the work of the ministry, for the edifying of the body of Christ" (Ephesians 4:11-12).

The "work of the ministry" involves soul winning, disciple making, encouraging, teaching Sunday School classes, and hundreds of other *jobs*. A Christianity that does not do the "work of the ministry" is not Christianity at all. When it comes to a choice between *playing* and *praying*, which do you usually choose? What does it take to keep you from attending the services of your local church? Is Sunday a *holy day* or a *holiday* for you? Is your Christianity a *vocation* or a *vacation*?

> One day I looked at myself,
> At the self that Christ can see;
> I saw the person I am today
> And the one I ought to be.
> I saw how little I really pray,
> How little I really do;
> I saw the influence of my life,
> How little of it was true!
>
> I saw the bundle of faults and fears
> I ought to lay on the shelf;
> I had given God a little bit,
> But I hadn't given myself.
> I came away from seeing myself,
> With my mind made up to be

The sort of person that Christ can use
With a heart He may always see!

Author Unknown

    Try to raise the level of your commitment to Christ each day of your life. Where has your commitment to Christ failed or where is it lacking? No one should ever walk away from a study of the Word of God the same as they were when they started. Commitment is a determination to do what you know is right and to be what you ought to be.

Handfuls On Purpose
Studies in the Book of Ruth
Chapter Four
Six Resolutions of Spiritual Commitment to Sanctification

1. List the six resolutions of commitment to Christ from Ruth 1:14-17 and explain what is practically involved in each one.

   A. "Whither thou goest, I will go."
   B. "Where thou lodgest, I will lodge."
   C. "Thy people shall be my people."
   D. "Thy God shall be my God."
   E. "Where thou diest, will I die."
   F. "If ought but death part thee and me."

2. What do you think is the greatest tragedy of the 20th century?

3. Why are so many people (who call themselves Christians) like Orpah?

4. What does the word "clave" mean in Ruth 1:14?

5. A commitment to <u>follow</u> Christ is a willingness that is prepared to drink of the _____ of His death. Few Christians are willing to _____ for Christ, let alone die for Him.

6. Read I John 1:3-7. What does a commitment to fellowship with Christ involve?

7. What did Ruth forsake in order to commit herself to the family of Naomi?

8. Read I John 3:10-19. What does a commitment to family involve according to these verses of Scripture?

9. Read II John 1:4-6 and III John 1:3-4. What does a commitment to family involve according to these verses of Scripture?

10. What two things do you need to recognize about a commitment to the Lordship of Christ?

11. How does Isaiah 1:2-3 describe many of today's professing Christians?

12. Read Luke 6:43-49 and John 8:31-37. What is a central aspect of what it means to commit to the Lordship of Christ?

13. After reading Acts 7:51-60 and understanding that Stephen knew the hostility the Jews had toward what he was going to say, would you consider him to be a *fanatic* for saying it, knowing they would probably kill him for doing so?
    A. Do you think that you would be willing to do the same thing in a similar circumstance?
    B. How would you measure your degree of fanaticism about your faith in Christ?

14. Philippians 3:8 defines the commitment of sacrifice of self. Do you think this verse describes your attitude and practice of life?

15. Read Ephesians 4:11-12. Describe some jobs meant by the "work of the ministry."

16. Read Romans 12:1-13. Discuss what these verses teach about the commitment to service (work)?

17. When it comes to a choice between PRAYING and PLAYING, which one do you choose?

18. Is Sunday a HOLY DAY or a HOLIDAY for you?

19. Is your Christianity a VOCATION or a VACATION?

20. From an eternal perspective, what will be the cause and effect results of your lack of biblical commitment on the eternal destinies (judgment, blessing and rewards) of all those whom God has put under your influence?

My Evaluation of My Commitments to Christ

On a scale of 1-10 (1 being the lowest and 10 being the highest level of commitment) rate your level of commitment to Christ in the following areas by what you <u>do</u>.

	1	2	3	4	5	6	7	8	9	10
1. I followed the Lord without reservations or restrictions this week.										
2. I seek to know Truth and walk in that Truth in order to fellowship.										
3. I confessed sin as soon as I recognized it in my life.										
4. My church family is important to me and I show it to them.										
5. I attended all the services of my local church this week.										
6. I did something to show someone I love them this week.										
7. I prayed for others this week.										
8. I studied God's Word and allowed the Spirit of God to speak to me.										
9. I stood apart from the crowd for Christ this week.										
10. A took a stand for righteousness before the world this week.										
11. My Christianity cost me something personal this week.										
12. I put out some Bible tracts this week.										
13. I personally gave someone a Bible tract this week.										
14. I personally tried to share the Gospel with someone this week.										
15. I was involved in some kind of soul winning visitation this week.										
16. I did some personal follow-up on someone who attended Church.										
17. I prayed for someone I knew was lost this week.										
18. I studied my Sunday School lesson this week.										
19. I did something to encourage another believer to serve the Lord.										
20. I sought the Lord's will in every matter of my daily life.										
21. I died to self each morning.										
22. I gave myself a living sacrifice to Christ each morning of this week										
23. I memorized at least one Scripture verse this week.										
24. I was aware of what God did for me this week and was thankful.										
25. Serving Christ was the most important thing in my life this week.										

Handfuls On Purpose
Studies in the Book of Ruth
Chapter Five
Full Surrender - The Open Door to Power with God

"¹ And Jacob went on his way, and the angels of God met him. ² And when Jacob saw them, he said, This *is* God's host: and he called the name of that place Mahanaim. {*that is, two hosts, or, camps*} ³ And Jacob sent messengers before him to Esau his brother unto the land of Seir, the country of Edom. ⁴ And he commanded them, saying, Thus shall ye speak unto my lord Esau; Thy servant Jacob saith thus, I have sojourned with Laban, and stayed there until now: ⁵ And I have oxen, and asses, flocks, and menservants, and womenservants: and I have sent to tell my lord, that I may find grace in thy sight. ⁶ And the messengers returned to Jacob, saying, We came to thy brother Esau, and also he cometh to meet thee, and four hundred men with him. ⁷ Then Jacob was greatly afraid and distressed: and he divided the people that *was* with him, and the flocks, and herds, and the camels, into two bands; ⁸ And said, If Esau come to the one company, and smite it, then the other company which is left shall escape. ⁹ And Jacob said, O God of my father Abraham, and God of my father Isaac, the LORD which saidst unto me, Return unto thy country, and to thy kindred, and I will deal well with thee: ¹⁰ I am not worthy of the least of all the mercies, and of all the truth, which thou hast shewed unto thy servant; for with my staff I passed over this Jordan; and now I am become two bands. ¹¹ Deliver me, I pray thee, from the hand of my brother, from the hand of Esau: for I fear him, lest he will come and smite me, *and* the mother with the children. ¹² And thou saidst, I will surely do thee good, and make thy seed as the sand of the sea, which cannot be numbered for multitude. ¹³ And he lodged there that same night; and took of that which came to his hand a present for Esau his brother; ¹⁴ Two hundred she goats, and twenty he goats, two hundred ewes, and twenty rams, ¹⁵ Thirty milch camels with their colts, forty kine, and ten bulls, twenty she asses, and ten foals. ¹⁶ And he delivered *them* into the hand of his servants, every drove by themselves; and said unto his servants, Pass over before me, and put a space betwixt drove and drove. ¹⁷ And he commanded the foremost, saying, When Esau my brother meeteth thee, and asketh thee, saying, Whose *art* thou? and whither goest thou? and whose *are* these before thee? ¹⁸ Then thou shalt say, *They be* thy servant Jacob's; it *is* a present sent unto my lord Esau: and, behold, also he *is* behind us. ¹⁹ And so commanded he the second, and the third, and all that followed the droves, saying, On this manner shall ye speak unto Esau, when ye find him. ²⁰ And say ye moreover, Behold, thy servant Jacob *is* behind us. For he said, I will appease him with the present that goeth before me, and afterward I will see his face; peradventure he will accept of me. ²¹ So went the present over before him: and himself lodged that night in the company. ²² And he rose up that night, and took his two wives, and his two womenservants, and his eleven sons, and passed over the ford Jabbok. ²³ And he took them, and sent them over the brook, and sent over that he had. ²⁴ And Jacob was left alone; and there wrestled a man with him until the breaking of the day. ²⁵ And when he saw that he prevailed not against him, he touched the hollow of his thigh; and the hollow of Jacob's thigh was out of joint, as he wrestled with him. ²⁶ And he said, Let me go, for the day breaketh. And he said, I will not let thee go, except thou bless me. ²⁷ And he said unto him, What *is* thy name? And he said, Jacob. ²⁸ And he said, Thy name shall be called no more Jacob, but Israel {*meaning a prince of God*}: for as a prince hast thou power with God and with men, and hast prevailed. ²⁹ And Jacob asked *him*, and said, Tell *me*, I pray thee, thy name. And he said, Wherefore *is* it *that* thou dost ask after my name? And he blessed him there. ³⁰ And Jacob called the name of the place Peniel {*meaning the face of God*}: for I have seen God face to face, and my life is preserved. ³¹ And as he passed over Penuel the sun rose upon him, and he halted upon his thigh. ³² Therefore the children of Israel eat not *of* the sinew which shrank, which *is* upon the hollow of the thigh, unto this day: because he touched the hollow of Jacob's thigh in the sinew that shrank" (Genesis 32:1-32).

    Many Christians (perhaps most Christians) live their lives without ever fully surrendering to the Lord (or even considering it). Either this is because of a degree of unbelief in their lives or they think full surrender is for some special order of Christians God calls to be pastors or missionaries. God wants full surrender from all Christians. This is the Bible doctrine of consecration. Consecration is what God does with fully surrendered Christians.

    Consecration is an important doctrine in the Bible because God only uses consecrated Christians. It is only the consecrated Christian who is filled with (controlled and empowered by) the Holy Spirit. Therefore, only the consecrated Christian will produce the fruit of the Spirit in his life. Consecration is the first step in what Christ refers to as abiding in Him in John chapter 15.

As we have studied the book of Ruth, it is interesting to hear how God uses circumstances and trials. God uses circumstances and trials to bring people to the place in their lives where they finally make the necessary commitments so that He can finally use them and empower them for service. Naomi and Ruth were such people. The same is true of this man Jacob in Genesis 32:1-32. That is why we will take a short excursion back to the time of Jacob.

Satan's world system is pulling every person in two directions. We are all being pulled towards the world (Satan's temptations to selfish and sinful living). We are all being pulled towards the Lord and the spiritual things of God and eternity. Because man is fallen in sin, man has a tendency (appetite) for the things of the world.

The person seeking to grow spiritually is working in partnership (fellowship) with the Holy Spirit to resist temptation and the pull of our flesh towards the things of this world. We can say that this person is *growing*. However, the person who is not striving to grow spiritually and is not resisting the temptations of this world will be simply carried along by the strong current with little resistance. We can say that person is just *flowing*.

Up to the point in time recorded in Genesis chapter thirty-two, Jacob was the latter kind of person. He was just *going with the flow*. He was deeply caught up in the things of the world and the lust of his flesh. In Genesis 32:1, we find Jacob doing just that, *going with the flow*. God says there of Jacob, "And Jacob went on his way."

Jacob's life was one of cunning and deceit. He learned the mastery of these works of his flesh at the apron strings of his mother Rebekah. There he learned the art of manipulation. In chapters thirty-one and thirty-two of Genesis, we find the turning point in Jacob's life. From this point forward, Jacob would be a different man. This turning point in Jacob's life revolves around a common denominator in the life of anyone ever used of God. A great Christian is not great because of how much he has of Christ (we all have an equal amount), but how much Christ has of him.

Many people have just enough *Christianity* to make them miserable. They attend church services, read their Bibles on occasion, and try to be all around good people. Yet there is a spiritual deadness about them. There is no joy in their Christianity.

The reason is simple. They have never stepped away from themselves long enough to make full surrender of their lives and to know what it really means to serve the Lord. God intends Christianity to be an open door to His power on our lives. For many, Christianity is nothing more than a closed up box of restraints of *do's* and *don'ts*. Until they get beyond all of that and really begin to become involved in helping people and working to rescue people from the *rapids of sin*, they will never grasp the reality of what is *Christianity*. They will never know the joy of seeing someone come to faith in Jesus Christ. They will never know the joy of seeing the weight of the burden of sin lifted from someone's shoulders. They will never experience the joy of knowing that some little boy or girl will no longer have to fear the beatings of a drunken mother or father because that parent has gotten saved.

Yet one of the saddest things about this kind of Christian is that he will never know the inner joy that comes to the heart that knows full surrender to Jesus Christ. He will never know the inner peace of being completely right with God. He will never know what it means to have the power of God on his life. Full surrender is to step away from this world and all the pseudo-security of places we have built for ourselves out of material things and to step into the empowering grace of God where He can use us.

Notice that God told Jacob (Genesis 31:11-13) to leave the household of Laban and to return to Bethel (the house of God). Jacob did not want to go there because Esau was there. All of Jacob's possessions were the things he had cheated Esau to get. In order for Jacob to be obedient to God, he had to go back to Bethel and take care of the matter of the past sin and deception he had been running away from for over twenty years (Genesis 31:38). In order to do so, he would have to leave the security and *safety net* of the world he had built to protect himself from his own brother and from the consequences of his deceptive life. However, in doing so he would also obey God for the first time in his life. He is immediately confronted with a crisis.

When you are *going with the flow*, Satan will not bother making things tough. When Jacob decided to do what was right, he turned around in the current and began to battle upstream. If you never confront your past and face up to the people you have failed, you will always be running away, locked into the prison of yesterday's failures. The moment you decide to begin doing things God's way, expect trouble. God did not promise to keep you from trouble. He promised to deliver you through it.

In Genesis chapter thirty-two, Jacob is about to learn a lesson every Christian needs to learn. If anyone wants to live for Christ and walk in obedience, it is essential to learn to live dependent upon Christ.

> "For therein is the righteousness of God revealed from faith to faith: as it is written, The just shall live by faith" (Romans 1:17).

> "But that no man is justified by the law in the sight of God, *it is* evident: for, The just shall live by faith" (Galatians 3:11).

> "Now the just shall live by faith: but if *any man* draw back, my soul shall have no pleasure in him" (Hebrews 10:38).

> "But without faith *it is* impossible to please *him*: for he that cometh to God must believe that he is, and *that* he is a rewarder of them that diligently seek him" (Hebrews 11:6).

Jacob is *scared to death* about doing what God expects of him. Full surrender will always take us to the limits of our faith. He thinks his brother is going to kill him. Has he believed God?

> "[11] Deliver me, I pray thee, from the hand of my brother, from the hand of Esau: for I fear him, lest he will come and smite me, *and* the mother with the children. [12] And thou saidst, I will surely do thee good, and make thy seed as the sand of the sea, which cannot be numbered for multitude" (Genesis 32:11-12).

Can God accomplish what He says in verse twelve if Jacob is dead? Jacob prays. However, it is obvious he is still not trusting God to deliver him.

> "And say ye moreover, Behold, thy servant Jacob *is* behind us. For he said, I will appease him with the present that goeth before me, and afterward I will see his face; peradventure he will accept of me" (Genesis 32:20).

Jacob is still manipulating, still playing politics, and still doing things the same old way. Jacob has still not learned the basics of spiritual living. He is over ninety years old and still in *spiritual Kindergarten.* We find a different (changed) man meeting Esau in Genesis chapter thirty-three. In chapter thirty-three, Jacob has been humbled. In chapter thirty-three, we find Jacob acknowledging his sin and seeking Esau's forgiveness and asking for mercy. Why did he change? What took place between Genesis 32:23 and Genesis 33:3? Jacob had a *close encounter* with God - an all-night wrestling match.

> "And Jacob was left alone; and there wrestled a man with him until the breaking of the day" (Genesis 32:24).

Jacob did not realize it, but this was finally the end of a lifetime of wrestling with God.

When you are in a wrestling match with God, you can never win until you surrender (and die to self). There are many Christians living their lives in a wrestling match with God and are not even aware of it. If that describes you, take a moment to understand what it took Jacob a lifetime to learn. The wrestling match you are fighting is a battle to the death. That night Jacob lost. The man *going with the flow* died and Israel (the man of God) was born.

The name Jacob (32:7) means *crooked heel catcher.* Jacob was a man who would do almost anything to have power with *men.* Now, after surrendering, he was a man who would have "power with God." That is what the name Israel means. It is only when you have real power with God that you have real power with men.

> "And he said, Thy name shall be called no more Jacob, but Israel {*meaning a prince of or with God*}: for as a prince hast thou power with God and with men, and hast prevailed" (Genesis 32:28).

In order for this all to take place, God had to change something about Jacob that would last for the rest of his life. It would be a physical change that would be a continual reminder of the day he wrestled with God and "prevailed."

> "[1] Then Jacob went on his journey, and came into the land of the people of the east. [2] And he looked, and behold a well in the field,

and, lo, there *were* three flocks of sheep lying by it; for out of that well they watered the flocks: and a great stone *was* upon the well's mouth. ³ And thither were all the flocks gathered: and they rolled the stone from the well's mouth, and watered the sheep, and put the stone again upon the well's mouth in his place. ⁴ And Jacob said unto them, My brethren, whence *be* ye? And they said, Of Haran *are* we. ⁵ And he said unto them, Know ye Laban the son of Nahor? And they said, We know *him*. ⁶ And he said unto them, *Is* he well? And they said, *He is* well: and, behold, Rachel his daughter cometh with the sheep. ⁷ And he said, Lo, *it is* yet high day, neither *is it* time that the cattle should be gathered together: water ye the sheep, and go *and* feed *them*. ⁸ And they said, We cannot, until all the flocks be gathered together, and *till* they roll the stone from the well's mouth; then we water the sheep. ⁹ And while he yet spake with them, Rachel came with her father's sheep: for she kept them. ¹⁰ And it came to pass, when Jacob saw Rachel the daughter of Laban his mother's brother, and the sheep of Laban his mother's brother, that Jacob went near, and rolled the stone from the well's mouth, and watered the flock of Laban his mother's brother" (Genesis 29:1-10).

According to Genesis 29:8, the stone that covered the mouth of the well was so large it required a group of shepherds to move it before they could water the sheep. However (according to Genesis 29:10), Jacob has enormously powerful legs and was able to move the stone by himself. In Jacob's wrestling match with God, God touched Jacob's thigh and took the strength of those legs away. From that moment on, Jacob never walked the same again (*physically* or *spiritually*). God wants people who walk by faith.

"³¹ And as he passed over Penuel the sun rose upon him, and he halted upon his thigh. ³² Therefore the children of Israel eat not *of* the sinew which shrank, which *is* upon the hollow of the thigh, unto this day: because he touched the hollow of Jacob's thigh in the sinew that shrank" (Genesis 32:31-32).

The new name Israel expresses the blessing of God (v. 26) upon a new walk of faith. Man's power *with* God is always directly proportionate to his faith in God and his surrender to God. At Bethel, Jacob was converted. Jacob was saved. At Bethel, Jacob learned that God was the Ruler of every place he would set his foot. However, at Jabbok (where Jacob wrestled with God), God became the ruler of Jacob by Jacob's choice.

Has God become the ruler of your life by your choice? It only happens when you fully surrender. Until then you are in a wrestling match with God. You will never win until you surrender. God becomes the ruler of your life when He has control of your heart and He will never take that control from you. You must willingly give Him control.

Pray this prayer from your heart. *Lord, I am yours - body, soul and spirit. All that I am, all I have and all I can be is yours to use as you see fit. If you want me to be a missionary, I will go. If you want me to be a preacher, I will preach. Where you want me to serve, I will serve. What you want me to give I will give. Whatever, wherever, and whenever, I am yours Father! Amen.*

Handfuls On Purpose
Studies in the Book of Ruth
Chapter Five
Full Surrender: The Open Door to Power with God

1. What are the two directions in which every person is being pulled?

2. From that perspective, are you *growing* or *flowing*?

3. What kind of man was Jacob before Genesis 32? Use one word to describe him.

4. Christianity is not how much you have of Christ, but how much He has of _____.

5. In Genesis 31:11-13, God told Jacob to leave the household of Laban at Haran and go back to Bethel. Why was that such a problem for Jacob according to Genesis 32:9-11?
    A. In order to go forward for Christ, we must learn to face our past with courage and faith. From that perspective, do you think full surrender (and the obedience to God that goes with it) will ever be easy?
    B. If you were going to measure the degree of a person's faith, would you find a more accurate measurement under a life of ease or adversity? Why is that true?

6. If you never confront your past and face the people you have failed, you will always be _____ away from your past.

7. When a Christian begins to take those *giant-steps* of obedience, what should he expect to happen?

8. What is absolutely essential to learn before a Christian will ever fully surrender to Christ and walk in obedience?
    A. From Genesis 32:12 we see the promise of God to Jacob. What does Jacob's fear reveal to us about the reality of his faith?
    B. Do you think Jacob really believed God for this promise?

9. Read Genesis 32:20. After Jacob asked God for deliverance from Esau's wrath, does he trust God for deliverance or does he revert to his old ways? What words reveal his attitude?

10. If you have never consciously, personally, and publicly surrendered your life fully to Christ, do you think you will be in a *wrestling match* with God until you do so?

11. From Genesis 32:27, was it Jacob or Israel that prevailed?
   A. Why is it important to distinguish between the old Jacob and the new man named Israel?
   B. What does the name *Jacob* mean?
   C. Does that describe Jacob's old character?
   D. What does the name *Israel* mean?
   E. Does that describe his new character and position with God?

12. From Genesis 29:1-10, what about Jacob did God have to change before Jacob would fully surrender?
   A. Will it take something like that in your life (some physical affliction) in order for you to surrender fully to Christ?
   B. With that physical affliction, could Jacob ever return to walking in his own strength again?

13. The new name Israel, expresses the blessing of God (32:26) on a walk of _____.

14. A person's power with God (and real power with men) is always directly proportionate to his _____ in God.

15. At Bethel, Jacob was converted (he was saved). At Bethel, Jacob learned that God was the real ruler of every place he would set his foot. At the river Jabbok, where Jacob wrestled with God, what did God finally become ruler of by Jacob's choice?

16. Surrendering to God is not giving *up*, but giving *in* to God. Before you can personally fully surrender to God, what areas of your life must you confront and deal with?

17. In salvation, God gives you His life (I John 5:11-12). When you fully surrender to Him, you surrender that new life to Him to use any way He sees fit. If you have trusted Jesus Christ with the eternal destiny of your soul, can you trust Him with the remaining years of this temporal lifetime?

18. Will you do that?

Handfuls On Purpose
Studies in the Book of Ruth
Chapter Six
The Pathway of Blessing through the Graveyard of Pride

"¹⁸ When she saw that she was stedfastly minded to go with her, then she left speaking unto her. ¹⁹ So they two went until they came to Bethlehem. And it came to pass, when they were come to Bethlehem, that all the city was moved about them, and they said, *Is* this Naomi? ²⁰ And she said unto them, Call me not Naomi {*meaning pleasant*}, call me Mara {*meaning bitter*}: for the Almighty hath dealt very bitterly with me. ²¹ I went out full, and the LORD hath brought me home again empty: why *then* call ye me Naomi, seeing the LORD hath testified against me, and the Almighty hath afflicted me? ²² So Naomi returned, and Ruth the Moabitess, her daughter in law, with her, which returned out of the country of Moab: and they came to Bethlehem in the beginning of barley harvest" (Ruth 1:18-22).

Most people make some kind of New Year's resolutions and plans for each New Year. They want to begin the New Year with renewed goals. This is going to be the year they finally do what they have wanted to accomplish for many preceding years, but have never gotten around to it. These people face the New Year excited by its potential. It is almost like getting a brand new start on life. It could be a new start, if it was not for the failures of the previous year that they will drag into the New Year like a *ball and chain*. We just cannot seem to escape some of these failures and struggles of life. Like unpaid bills and broken relationships, they just continue to haunt us.

We can only start new when we are willing to confront our past failures directly and begin to deal with the behavioral problems that caused them. Otherwise, new starts always conclude with the same old endings.

A zoo was preparing a new Polar Bear exhibit. The zoo intended to have a big, beautiful, and natural environment built when the Polar Bear arrived. However, when the Polar Bear got there, it was not finished. Therefore, they put a cage in the middle of this new area until the environment was completed. The cage was just large enough for the bear to take three paces one way, stand up, turn around, and take three paces back. For six months, that is how that Polar Bear lived. When the workers finally completed the natural environment all around the cage, they removed the cage. What do you suppose the Polar Bear did? That is right - three paces one direction, stand up, turn around, and then three paces in the other direction.

Sometimes we unknowingly establish patterns of living that are harmful to us. God is actively involved in our lives to change those harmful behavior patterns. Sometimes the pathways are beaten in and become hardened. That is where we pick up our story in the book of Ruth.

Naomi (typical of backslidden Israel) has disobeyed God, moved to Moab, and there her husband has died. Her two sons marry Moabite sisters and die in Moab. Naomi decides to return to Bethlehemjudah because God's chastisement of famine is over. Even though this family tried to escape God's chastisement, they could not. God was intent on change - not just a change in action, but also a change of heart (motivation).

According to Ruth 1:13, Naomi had filled herself with bitterness toward God over what had happened to her. She recognized that what had happened came from the chastising "hand of God." She was not yet willing to recognize why God's hand of chastisement was upon her. She had a broken heart due to the conditions of her chastisement, but her heart was not yet changed. She was yet unwilling to face up to the cause of her chastisement. She (Israel) had sinned. She was not yet repentant about it. Otherwise, she would not have been bitter about it. God's chastisement was about to lead her back to the place she was supposed to be, but her heart was still in Moab (in rebellion). God removed the cage, but she still needed to be deal with patterns of life that got her in trouble. God will begin to show her the blessing of obedience to His Word, even in adversity.

Naomi gives up trying to convince Ruth to stay in Moab (Ruth 1:18). Naomi's mindset is still earthbound and temporal. This has always been Israel's main spiritual problem. It is obvious that Naomi's pride is still motivating her.

Why do you suppose Naomi did not want to take these Moabite women back to Bethlehem with her? Ruth and Orpah would be a walking testimony to Naomi's (Israel's) disobedience to

God. Pride not only can motivate us to do some foolish things, pride can keep us from doing the right thing. Pride is not a character attribute. Pride is part of our sin nature and we need to recognize it for what it is - a motivator to sin. One of the central purposes of God's chastisement is to break the stranglehold pride has on our lives.

> "[14] But if ye will not hearken unto me, and will not do all these commandments; [15] And if ye shall despise my statutes, or if your soul abhor my judgments, so that ye will not do all my commandments, *but* that ye break my covenant: [16] I also will do this unto you; I will even appoint over {*upon*} you terror, consumption, and the burning ague {*fever*}, that shall consume the eyes, and cause sorrow of heart: and ye shall sow your seed in vain, for your enemies shall eat it. [17] And I will set my face against you, and ye shall be slain before your enemies: they that hate you shall reign over you; and ye shall flee when none pursueth you. [18] And if ye will not yet for all this hearken unto me, then I will punish you seven times more for your sins. [19] And I will break the pride of your power; and I will make your heaven as iron, and your earth as brass: [20] And your strength shall be spent in vain: for your land shall not yield her increase, neither shall the trees of the land yield their fruits" (Leviticus 26:14-20).

The United States stands upon the brink of a similar experience with God. When God says, "I will make your heaven as iron" (v. 19), He is referring to a rainless sky. When God says He would make "your earth as brass" (v. 19), He is referring to a barren, crop less ground. Together these two things result in famine because the ground produces no food.

God says the purpose of this chastisement was to break the "pride of your power," or the *holding power of pride*. When Ruth 1:1 says, "there was famine in the land," God is telling us His intent was breaking the *holding power of the pride* of Israel that kept her from admitting her sin before God and others (repentance).

Pride is at the root of most sin and pride is the sin that keeps so many people from God's blessing and fellowship (even from being saved).

> "[1] Why standest thou afar off, O LORD? *why* hidest thou *thyself* in times of trouble? [2] The wicked in *his* pride doth persecute the poor:

let them be taken in the devices that they have imagined. ³ For the wicked boasteth of his heart's desire, and blesseth the covetous, *whom* the LORD abhorreth {*blesseth . . . : or, the covetous blesseth himself, he abhorreth the LORD*}. ⁴ The wicked, through the pride of his countenance, will not seek *after God*: God *is* not in all his thoughts. {*God is....: or, all his thoughts are, there is no God*} ⁵ His ways are always grievous; thy judgments *are* far above out of his sight: *as for* all his enemies, he puffeth at them. ⁶ He hath said in his heart, I shall not be moved: for *I shall* never *be* in adversity. ⁷ His mouth is full of cursing and deceit and fraud: under his tongue *is* mischief and vanity {*iniquity*}. ⁸ He sitteth in the lurking places of the villages: in the secret places doth he murder the innocent: his eyes are privily set against the poor. ⁹ He lieth in wait secretly {*lit.; in the secret places*} as a lion in his den: he lieth in wait to catch the poor: he doth catch the poor, when he draweth him into his net. ¹⁰ He croucheth, *and* humbleth himself, that the poor may fall by his strong ones. ¹¹ He hath said in his heart, God hath forgotten: he hideth his face; he will never see *it*" (Psalm 10:1-11).

God cannot be in any of the thoughts of the person filled with pride because pride fills us with our self until there is room for nothing else.

"*When* pride cometh, then cometh shame: but with the lowly *is* wisdom" (Proverbs 11:2).

This is where Naomi is in this part of the book of Ruth. She is filled with pride and shame is at the threshold of her life (Ruth 1:19).

"So they two went until they came to Bethlehem. And it came to pass, when they were come to Bethlehem, that all the city was moved about them, and they said, *Is* this Naomi (Ruth 1:19)?"

The last "they" in Ruth 1:19 is in the feminine gender. "They" refers to the other women of Bethlehem, Naomi's peers. "They" say, "Is this Naomi?" Naomi had been a woman of wealth and influence, but now she is a widow without children. This was the worst state of destitution in which a Jewish woman could find herself. To make the matters even worse, she has a Gentile daughter-in-law with her as a testimony to the disobedience of her sons.

These women of Bethlehem remembered Naomi as a beautiful rose in an expensive vase. Now the rose has withered and the vase is tarnished and cracked. Pride brought her to the place of shame, but this was a good place to be if you look at her circumstances from God's perspective. It is here, in the time of shame that God brings pride to its knees in humility before Him and others. Pride is a yoke of bondage that shame forces us to confront and deal with. When a person struggles to keep his pride, he is actually struggling against the work of God in his life because God is working in our lives to remove pride. **Pride is one of the three central sources of sin.**

"For all that *is* in the world, the lust of the flesh, and the lust of the eyes, and the pride of life, is not of the Father, but is of the world" (I John 2:16).

God uses chastisement to bring pride to shame. God uses shame to bring the prideful sinner to humility. Only the humbled will be willing to acknowledge (confess) their sin publicly.

"[20] And she said unto them, Call me not Naomi, call me Mara: for the Almighty hath dealt very bitterly with me. [21] I went out full, and the LORD hath brought me home again empty: why *then* call ye me Naomi, seeing the LORD hath testified against me, and the Almighty hath afflicted me" (Ruth 1:20-21)?

Proud people will refuse to acknowledge their failures before anyone. Just like the Polar Bear, even when they remove the cage of chastisement, proud people will continue in the same old pattern of bondage. Before genuine repentance can ever come, prideful people must confront the issue of their pride head on. Before anyone will ever deal with the pride in his life, the circumstances necessary to recognize pride as harmful and sinful must enable him to recognize pride for what it is.

The pathway to blessing always goes through the gateway of humility and into the graveyard of pride. The very root of arrogance and pride is our refusal to consider God's will and respond to Him biblically. Instead, the arrogant, prideful person just goes on his way thinking God will accept and bless him apart from an obedient relationship with Him.

Pride is usually the *fountainhead* of all quarreling, jealousy, anger, factions, slander, gossip, and most other sins of this nature. The great difficulty in ever dealing with the sin of pride is that pride refuses to allow us to even look at it as the source of a problem. Pride is a stubborn and arrogant *alter ego* that bullies and manipulates us into always looking somewhere else or at someone else. Isaiah 14:12-15 informs us that it was Satan's pride that caused his fall into sin.

"[12] How art thou fallen from heaven, O Lucifer {*or, O Day Star*}, son of the morning! *how* art thou cut down to the ground, which didst weaken the nations! [13] For thou hast said in thine heart, I will ascend into heaven, I will exalt my throne above the stars of God: I will sit also upon the mount of the congregation, in the sides of the north: [14] I will ascend above the heights of the clouds; I will be like the most High. [15] Yet thou shalt be brought down to hell, to the sides of the pit" (Isaiah 14:12-15).

Therefore, pride is the root cause of all evil and all sin.

"[4] And the serpent said unto the woman, Ye shall not surely die: [5] For God doth know that in the day ye eat thereof, then your eyes shall be opened, and ye shall be as gods, knowing good and evil. [6] And when the woman saw that the tree *was* good for food, and that it *was* pleasant to the eyes, and a tree to be desired to make *one* wise, she took of the fruit thereof, and did eat, and gave also unto her husband with her; and he did eat" (Genesis 3:4-6).

The only means to overcoming the crippling sin of pride is to accept God's crutch of humility. Either we see ourselves stumbling in the darkness and humble ourselves before God, or God will humble us with chastisement and shame. He will do that because He cannot bless us and use us until we deal with the sin of pride in our lives.

"And whosoever shall exalt himself shall be abased; and he that shall humble himself shall be exalted" (Matthew 23:12).

The word "abased" is from the Greek word *tapeinoo* (tap-i-no'-o). It means *to be brought low*. The idea is that the person who lifts himself up in pride will be humiliated or brought down in shame. The person who humbles (same word, *tapeinoo*) himself, God will exalt to a position of prominence. James says almost the same thing.

> "Humble yourselves in the sight of the Lord, and he shall lift you up" (James 4:10).

Always have pity on proud people. Their arrogance is destined for the humbling hand of God on their lives just as it was on Naomi's life. It is not a matter of *if*. It is a matter of *when*. I Peter 5:5-7 gives us wise instruction on how to escape the prison of our own pride. We would be wise to listen and obey.

> "[5] Likewise, ye younger, submit yourselves unto the elder. Yea, all *of you* be subject one to another, and be clothed with humility: for God resisteth the proud, and giveth grace to the humble. [6] Humble yourselves therefore under the mighty hand of God, that he may exalt you in due time: [7] Casting all your care upon him; for he careth for you. [8] Be sober, be vigilant; because your adversary the devil, as a roaring lion, walketh about, seeking whom he may devour: [9] Whom resist stedfast in the faith, knowing that the same afflictions are accomplished in your brethren that are in the world" (I Peter 5:5-9).

If we want to succeed in our commitments to Christ and our resolutions to change, we will need to learn to humble ourselves before the Lord. If you will not do that, I Peter 5:8 applies especially to you. Expect your life to be *lion meat*. Lions attack the lame and crippled first. Pride cripples the person who refuses to deal with pride as sin. That person should just hang a sign around his neck - *LION MEAT*.

Handfuls On Purpose
Studies in the Book of Ruth
Chapter Six
The Pathway of Blessing through the Graveyard of Pride

1. According to Ruth 1:21, what was Naomi "full" of when she "went out"?

2. What was she "empty" of when the Lord brought her "home again"?

3. If we are not willing to confront our past failures head on and begin to deal with the behavioral problems that caused them, how will all *new beginnings* conclude?

4. According to Ruth 1:13, what was Naomi's attitude toward the LORD for His attempts at changing her heart through chastisement? Was she still acting in pride?

5. According to Ruth 1:18, what was probably the central reason why Naomi did not want Ruth to go back to Bethlehem with her?

6. From Leviticus 26:19, what was God's intent in his chastisement here?

7. What two things does pride keep us from in our relationship with God?
    A. BL _ _ _ _ _ G
    B. FEL _ _ _ _ _ _ P

8. From Psalm 10:4, why is God not in <u>ANY</u> of the thoughts of the prideful?

9. According to Proverbs 11:2, what will always be the end result of pride in a person's life?
    A. Compare your answer to Ruth 1:19. Was this the result of Naomi's pride?
    B. Is shame a bad thing if it accomplishes its purpose?
    C. Can shame and pride exist together in a person's life?
    D. What is the only reason shame can continue to exist?

10. From I John 2:16, what are the three central sources of all temptation and sin?

11. What happens in Ruth 1:20-21 to show that Naomi was humbled?

12. What is the great difficulty in dealing with our pride?

13. Does pride ever recognize itself, even when it is obvious to everyone else?

14. According to Matthew 23:12, what is God's solution to pride?
    A. Do you regularly practice this?
    B. Today, will you decide to make this a regular practice of your life?
    C. Have you ever considered yourself to be *lion meat*?

Handfuls On Purpose
Studies in the Book of Ruth
Chapter Seven
Christ: Our Kinsman Redeemer

"And Naomi had a kinsman of her husband's; a mighty man of wealth, of the family of Elimelech; and his name *was* Boaz" (Ruth 2:1).

In Ruth 2:1, God introduces us to the next character in the story of Ruth. His name is Boaz. The name Boaz means *in him is strength*. The meaning of the name refers specifically to the ability to redeem. Boaz is a type of Christ.

As we look at Boaz, we will see him as a type of Christ our Redeemer, who redeems out of love and grace rather than law and duty. Ruth represents every Christian as an individual and she represents the Church corporately. As the Church corporately, she is the Bride of Christ. Through the redemption of Ruth and Naomi, we will see how Christ fulfilled the law in our redemption.

In this chapter, we want to look at the extremes Jesus (the eternal Son of God) went in order to provide redemption to "whosoever will." Leviticus chapter twenty-five tells us there were four basic requirements of the law before a Redeemer could redeem the lost estate of a family member. It is in the fulfillment of these four requirements that we so evidently see the extremes of God's love for us. These fulfillments provide very rich truths for us.

Requirement One - a redeemer must be a *kinsman* (Leviticus 25:48-49).

"[48] After that he is sold he may be redeemed again; one of his brethren may redeem him: [49] Either his uncle, or his uncle's son, may redeem him, or *any* that is nigh of kin unto him of his family may redeem him; or if he be able, he may redeem himself" (Leviticus 25:48-49).

In this requirement, God reminds us of one of the most remarkable truths in the Bible. In order to redeem fallen humanity from the bondage of sin, the eternal Son of God became one of us. He became a man.

"³ Even so we, when we were children, were in bondage under the elements of the world: ⁴ But when the fulness of the time was come, God sent forth his Son, made of a woman, made under the law, ⁵ To redeem them that were under the law, that we might receive the adoption of sons" (Galatians 4:3-5).

The words "fullness of time" take us all the way back to Genesis 3:15 where God made His first promise of a Redeemer.

"And I will put enmity between thee and the woman, and between thy seed and her seed; it shall bruise thy head, and thou shalt bruise his heel" (Genesis 3:15).

The emphasis of the "fullness of time" is that God made the creation pregnant with the promise of a Redeemer. In the birth of Jesus, the time of delivery came to full term. God became a man through the common means of conception (yet uncommon in that it was an immaculate conception) and human birth (yet uncommon in that it was a virgin birth). The fact of incarnation is the most wonderful example of selfless love ever known to humanity.

"⁵ Let this mind be in you, which was also in Christ Jesus: ⁶ Who, being in the form of God, thought it not robbery to be equal with God: ⁷ But made himself of no reputation, and took upon him the form of a servant, and was made in the likeness of men: ⁸ And being found in fashion as a man, he humbled himself, and became obedient unto death, even the death of the cross" (Philippians 2:5-8).

The words "form of God" inform us that Jesus Christ was an eternal, spiritual Being who transcended time and space, is without a beginning or and ending, is omnipotent, omnipresent, and omniscient. The words "thought it not robbery" reveal to us that the eternal Son of God did not selfishly cling to His Godhood.
The words "of no reputation" reveal that the eternal Son of God emptied Himself of the prestige of His Godhood to become a common man without position, or reputation. The words "was made" refer to His conception and birth. The words "in the likeness of men" refers to His becoming one of humanity ("men" is plural).
We have no way of comprehending what it means to be God. Therefore, we have no way of comprehending the enormous love and sacrifice of the eternal Son of God when He became man. The

Creator became part of His creation. What incomprehensible love.

Requirement Two - a redeemer must be *able* to pay the price of redemption (Leviticus 25:25-28).

"^{25} If thy brother be waxen poor, and hath sold away *some* of his possession, and if any of his kin come to redeem it, then shall he redeem that which his brother sold. ^{26} And if the man have none to redeem it, and himself be able to redeem it; ^{27} Then let him count the years of the sale thereof, and restore the overplus unto the man to whom he sold it; that he may return unto his possession. ^{28} But if he be not able to restore *it* to him, then that which is sold shall remain in the hand of him that hath bought it until the year of jubile: and in the jubile it shall go out, and he shall return unto his possession" (Leviticus 25:25-28).

God's Word says that Boaz (Ruth 2:1) was a "mighty man of wealth." Boaz was able to pay the price of redemption. Christ fulfills this requirement in that He was able to pay God's price of redemption. God's price of redemption was the shedding of innocent blood.

"And almost all things are by the law purged with blood; and without shedding of blood is no remission" (Hebrews 9:22).

"^{18} Forasmuch as ye know that ye were not redeemed with corruptible things, *as* silver and gold {*a broad term referring to all the religious rituals of the Temple*}, from your vain conversation {*manner of life, meaning empty attempts at self-righteousness*} *received* by tradition from your fathers {*they did not come from God*}; ^{19} But {*you are redeemed*} with the precious blood of Christ, as of a lamb without blemish and without spot " (I Peter 1:18-19).

God's demand for blood of a sinless innocent as the price of redemption meant that Christ our Redeemer must die in order to redeem us from the bondage of sin.

"^{25} Nor yet that he should offer himself often, as the high priest entereth into the holy place every year with blood of others; ^{26} For then must he often have suffered since the foundation of the world: but now once in the end of the world hath he appeared to put away sin by the sacrifice of himself. ^{27} And as it is appointed unto men once to die, but after this the judgment: [28] So Christ was once offered to bear the sins of many; and unto them that look for him shall he appear the second time without sin unto salvation" (Hebrews 9:25-28).

We cannot fathom the enormous cost of our redemption, nor can we fathom the statement of Christ in the Garden of Gethsemane when He said, "Nevertheless not my will, but thine, be done" (Luke 22:42).

Requirement Three - he must be *willing* to redeem (Leviticus 25:35).

"And if thy brother be waxen poor, and fallen in decay with thee; then thou shalt relieve him: *yea, though he be* a stranger, or a sojourner; that he may live with thee" (Leviticus 25:35).

Jesus Christ was willing to do what humanity needed to redeem us from our lost state of existence.

"[4] For *it is* not possible that the blood of bulls and of goats should take away sins. [5] Wherefore when he cometh into the world, he saith, Sacrifice and offering thou wouldest not, but a body hast thou prepared me: [6] In burnt offerings and *sacrifices* for sin thou hast had no pleasure. [7] Then said I, Lo, I come (in the volume of the book it is written of me,) to do thy will, O God. [8] Above when he said, Sacrifice and offering and burnt offerings and *offering* for sin thou wouldest not, neither hadst pleasure *therein*; which are offered by the law; [9] Then said he, Lo, I come to do thy will, O God. He taketh away the first, that he may establish the second. [10] By the which will we are sanctified through the offering of the body of Jesus Christ once *for all*" (Hebrews 10:4-10).

The words "by the which will" in Hebrews 10:10 refer to both God's will and the will of Jesus. Their wills were one (the same). Why was our redemption God's will? Why would Jesus be willing to pay such an enormous price to redeem lost humanity? There is only one answer - because He loves us with a love that goes beyond human comprehension.

"For God so loved the world, that he gave his only begotten Son, that whosoever believeth in him should not perish, but have everlasting life" (John 3:16).

Stop and think about this verse for a moment. Think about what it means when it says, "God so loved . . . that He gave His only begotten Son." There is no greater love than this. Open yourself to it. The love of God is so great. He extends His loving hand of redemption to everyone and anyone, even to those shaking their fist in His face with every sin.

God's love separated the sin from the sinner and laid the sin upon His Son at Calvary paying the wages of every sin humanity would ever commit (Romans 3:23 and 1 John 2:2). In that the wages of sin were paid by the shedding of the Blood of Christ, God offers salvation as a gift of His grace to whosoever will believe the Gospel and acknowledge Jesus to be Lord (Romans 10:9-13).

Requirement Four - he must be free from the need of redemption himself (Ruth 4:4-6).

Jesus did not need redemption because He was both holy and sinless.

"^{34} Then said Mary unto the angel, How shall this be, seeing I know not a man? ^{35} And the angel answered and said unto her, The Holy Ghost shall come upon thee, and the power of the Highest shall overshadow thee: therefore also that holy thing which shall be born of thee shall be called the Son of God" (Luke 1:34-35).

Jesus was no ordinary man. He was unique. He was holy and sinless. Yet, He can identify with every temptation and weakness of mankind.

"For we have not an high priest which cannot be touched with the feeling of our infirmities; but was in all points tempted like as *we are, yet* without sin" (Hebrews 4:15).

This holy and sinless God/man was executed for the sins of humanity as our substitute, the godly for the ungodly.

"^{6} For when we were yet without strength, in due time Christ died for the ungodly. ^{7} For scarcely for a righteous man will one die: yet peradventure for a good man some would even dare to die ^{8} But God commendeth his love toward us, in that, while we were yet sinners, Christ died for us" (Romans 5:6-8).

"While we were yet sinners" - lost in our sin and condemned to eternal death, shaking our rebellious fists in the face of God with every transgression, the sinless One (Jesus the Christ) "died for us." Knowing all this, what must we do to be redeemed?

"^{13} Christ hath redeemed us from the curse of the law, being made a curse for us: for it is written, Cursed *is* every one that hangeth on a tree: ^{14} That the blessing of Abraham might come on the Gentiles through Jesus Christ; that we might receive the promise of the Spirit through faith" (Galatians 3:13-14).

Christ's redemption made salvation available. God offers salvation as a gift.

"^{4} But God, who is rich in mercy, for his great love wherewith he loved us, ^{5} Even when we were dead in sins, hath quickened us together with Christ, (**by** grace ye are saved;) {*by whose grace*} ^{6} And hath raised *us* up together, and made *us* sit together in heavenly *places* in Christ Jesus: ^{7} That in the ages to come he might shew the exceeding riches of his grace in *his* kindness toward us through Christ Jesus. ^{8} For by grace are ye saved through faith; and that not of yourselves: *it is* the gift of God: ^{9} Not of works, lest any man should boast" (Ephesians 2:4-9).

Have you received the wonderful gift of God's grace? Have you received the gift of salvation in the gift of a Saviour? Salvation is in a Person. You need to receive the eternal Son of God, Jesus Christ, into your life. He is only your Kinsman Redeemer if you receive Him.

"^{11} He came unto his own, and his own received him not. ^{12} But as many as received him, to them gave he **power** {*the right, or privilege*} to become the sons of God, *even* to them that believe on his name:" (John 1:11-12).

"Neither is there salvation in any other: for there is none other name under heaven given among men, whereby we must be saved" (Acts 4:12).

Handfuls On Purpose
Studies in the Book of Ruth
Chapter Seven
Christ: Our Kinsman Redeemer

1. What does the name Boaz mean?

2. Who does Ruth represent individually?

3. Who does Ruth represent corporately?

4. List the four requirements of a Redeemer.
   A. A Redeemer must be a _____.
   B. A Redeemer must be _____ to pay the price of redemption.
   C. A Redeemer must be _____ to redeem.
   D. A Redeemer must be free from the _____ of redemption himself.

5. Read Galatians 4:4-5. In order to redeem mankind from the bondage of sin, what did God need to become?

6. Looking back to Genesis 3:15, God's creation was made *pregnant* with the promise of Messiah. From Galatians 4:4, how does the "fullness of time" relate to that promise?

7. Read Philippians 2:5-7. Explain the following phrases:
   A. "Form of God"
   B. "Thought it not robbery"
   C. "Of no reputation"
   D. "Was made"

8. Read Hebrews 9:22. What was the price God put on redemption?

9. Read I Peter 1:18-19. What did that mean Jesus must do to pay that price?
   A. Do you realize He did that for <u>you</u>?
   B. According to Hebrews 9:25-28, how many times did Christ have to pay the price of redemption?
   C. If some forms of Christianity teach that Christ must be continually offered as a sacrifice in *Holy Communion* - does that establish or deny the sufficiency of His redemption?
   D. Do you believe that He was able to redeem you?

10. Read Hebrews 10:4-10. According to verse 7, what does the whole of Scripture reveal to us about the purpose of Christ's coming?
   A. According to verse 10, whose will was "the which will"?
   B. Was Jesus willing to redeem you?

11. Why would Christ be willing to pay such an enormous price to redeem us (see John 3:16)?

12. What two things must we try to comprehend before we will ever be able to comprehend the depth of God's love for us?

13. Read Luke 1:35. What does the word "holy" signify to you about Jesus Christ?

14. Read Hebrews 4:15. Why can Jesus identify with the "feeling" of our sinful weaknesses?

15. From Hebrews 4:15, what is unique about Jesus' temptation that cannot be said of any other human being?

16. Read Romans 5:6-8. According to verse 6, who are the "ungodly"?

17. What were the "ungodly . . . without" that necessitated Jesus dying for them?

18. According to Galatians 3:13-14, through what means do we "receive the promise of the Spirit"?

19. Have you personally received the free gift of God's redemption in Jesus Christ?

20. Read Ephesians 2:8-9. What is the *hand* (means) by which we receive the free gift of God's salvation "by grace"?

21. Read John 1:11-12. What can anyone call himself who has received the "power" (authority) to do so because he has received Jesus Christ?

Handfuls On Purpose
Studies in the Book of Ruth
Chapter Eight
Seven Character Traits of a Person with a Servant's Heart

"[22] So Naomi returned, and Ruth the Moabitess, her daughter in law, with her, which returned out of the country of Moab: and they came to Bethlehem in the beginning of barley harvest. . . [1] And Naomi had a kinsman of her husband's, a mighty man of wealth, of the family of Elimelech; and his name *was* Boaz. [2] And Ruth the Moabitess said unto Naomi, Let me now go to the field, and glean ears of corn after *him* in whose sight I shall find grace. And she said unto her, Go, my daughter. [3] And she went, and came, and gleaned in the field after the reapers: and her hap was to light on a part of the field *belonging* unto Boaz, who *was* of the kindred of Elimelech" (Ruth 1:22-2:3).

We have all heard of someone described as a person with a servant's heart. That is an admirable character quality. It is a central characteristic of a yielded and mature Christian. It was certainly the character of Ruth.

We pick up our story in Ruth 1:22. It is barley season in Bethlehem. That means it was early spring. Naomi and Ruth are back in Bethlehem, bankrupt and destitute. The only thing keeping them from starvation is God's provision in the Law giving them the right to glean.

"[9] And when ye reap the harvest of your land, thou shalt not wholly reap the corners of thy field, neither shalt thou gather the gleanings of thy harvest. [10] And thou shalt not glean thy vineyard, neither shalt thou gather *every* grape of thy vineyard; thou shalt leave them for the poor and stranger: I *am* the LORD your God" (Leviticus 19:9-10).

In this chapter, we want to concentrate on the character of Ruth, revealed by her attitude towards gleaning as a servant. We need to review what happened to Naomi to prepare her and Ruth to be used of God (Ruth 1:21). Naomi "went out full" of wealth and pride and came home broken and "empty" of wealth and pride.

Before God can use any one of us fully as He wants too, we must empty ourselves of pride. Pride is the essence of our sin nature (self). Before the Holy Spirit can fill us, we must be emptied of self.

Our bodies are the Temple of the Holy Spirit (He dwells within us), but He cannot fill us with the power of His glory when our "flesh" (self) is on the throne of our life (control).

We must die to selfish pride and give Jesus the Throne of our lives (control). This is the central reason why so few Christians never realize the potential that is theirs in accomplishing things for Jesus Christ. They attempt to serve God while remaining in the "flesh" (refusing to relinquish the *steering wheel* of their lives to God).

In this chapter, we will look at seven characteristics of a servant's heart. The Spirit of God can only produce each of these seven characteristics when the believer dies to self and yields control of his life to the indwelling Holy Spirit.

> "I am crucified with Christ: nevertheless I live; yet not I, but Christ liveth in me: and the life which I now live in the flesh I live by the faith of the Son of God, who loved me, and gave himself for me" (Galatians 2:20).

Everyone wants to lead. Few want to follow. Wanting leadership is about wanting control. God only allows those to lead who understand what it means to follow (yield control). When we talk about being "filled with the Holy Spirit," the central idea is yielding control. The Holy Spirit will not empower us if we have not yielded to Him. God wants each of us to learn to trust Him with the control of our lives by yielding control to Him. Yielding is a choice to be His servant so that God can use us to lead others. This is central to the Lordship of Jesus Christ and central to the principle of service.

> "[27] And whosoever will be chief among you, let him be your servant: [28] Even as the Son of man came not to be ministered unto, but to minister, and to give his life a ransom for many" (Matthew 20:27-28).

> "[11] Likewise reckon ye also yourselves to be dead indeed unto sin, but alive unto God through Jesus Christ our Lord. [12] Let not sin therefore reign in your mortal body, that ye should obey it in the lusts thereof. [13] Neither yield ye your members *as* **instruments** of unrighteousness unto sin: but yield yourselves unto God, as those that are alive from the dead, and your members *as* **instruments** of

righteousness unto God" {***instruments:*** *Gr. arms, or, weapons*} (Romans 6:11-13).

We find the first characteristic of a servant's heart in the words, "Let me now go to the field" (Ruth 2:2). This reveals the character of yieldedness or submissiveness.

> "[18] And be not drunk with wine, wherein is excess; but be filled with the Spirit; [19] Speaking to yourselves in psalms and hymns and spiritual songs, singing and making melody in your heart to the Lord; [20] Giving thanks always for all things unto God and the Father in the name of our Lord Jesus Christ; [21] <u>Submitting yourselves</u> one to another in the fear of God" (Ephesians 5:18-21).

No one will submit himself to serving others until he has yielded all that he has and all that he is to serving Jesus Christ.
The second characteristic of a servant's heart is humility. Ruth was willing to glean. Have you ever noticed there are certain kinds of work some people think they are just too good to do?
The opposite of humility is pride. Satan tries to fool us into thinking pride is something good to have. We are deceived into thinking that if we would lose our pride, we would also lose our dignity. The very opposite is true. We have no dignity in God's eyes until we lose our pride. Pride defiles us before God.

> "The fear of the LORD *is* the instruction of wisdom; and before **honour** {*dignity*} *is* humility" (Proverbs 15:33).

> "**By** {*by the reward of humility*} humility *and* the fear of the LORD *are* riches, and **honour** {*dignity*}, and life" (Proverbs 22:4).

Luke said the following about the Apostle Paul:

> "Serving the Lord with all humility of mind, and with many tears, and temptations, which befell me by the lying in wait of the Jews:" (Acts 20:19).

The third characteristic of a servant's heart is spiritual ambition. Ruth not only was willing to go "to the field," she wanted to go. The biblical word for ambition is the word *zeal* or *zealous*. God commands every Christian to be "zealous." The rebuke of Revelation 3:19 was because the Christians of the church (period of church history) of Laodicea had no spiritual ambition.

> "As many as I love, I rebuke and chasten: be zealous therefore, and repent" (Revelation 3:19).

Spiritual ambition is much different from worldly ambition. Spiritual ambition is intent on bringing glory and praise to God, not self. In fact, spiritual ambition is almost offended when given praise for something God has done through our lives. Spiritual ambition immediately re-directs any praise to God (where it belongs). Spiritual ambition is more than a willingness to do the work of the ministry. It is a drive to do the work of the ministry. The motivation of real spiritual ambition is that when the work is done (and done excellently), people will praise God.

When the Holy Spirit convicts us about a failure to do the work of the ministry and we yield to Him about that, we should not confuse that yielding to do the work with actually doing the work. A *decision* to the work is not the same as *doing it*. Every employer knows that some people come to *work*, while others just *come* to work. Those with a servant's heart come to *work* (emphasize on work, not just coming).

The fourth characteristic of a servant's heart is consideration. Being consciously aware of and considerate of the needs of others is central to a servant's heart. Ruth went to glean because she wanted to provide for the needs of Naomi as well as herself. A servant who never does the work of the ministry is nothing more than a leech on the body of Christ.

> "[23] Let us hold fast the profession of *our* faith without wavering; (for he *is* faithful that promised;) [24] And let us consider one another to provoke unto love and to good works: [25] Not forsaking the assembling of ourselves together, as the manner of some *is*; but exhorting *one another*: and so much the more, as ye see the day approaching" (Hebrews 10:23-25).

We best teach others to be servants by example. When Jesus wanted to teach His disciples what it means to serve, what did He do? He washed their feet.

"⁴ He riseth from supper, and laid aside his garments; and took a towel, and girded himself. ⁵ After that he poureth water into a bason, and began to wash the disciples' feet, and to wipe *them* with the towel wherewith he was girded. ⁶ Then cometh he to Simon Peter: and Peter saith unto him, Lord, dost thou wash my feet? ⁷ Jesus answered and said unto him, What I do thou knowest not now; but thou shalt know hereafter. ⁸ Peter saith unto him, Thou shalt never wash my feet. Jesus answered him, If I wash thee not, thou hast no part with me. ⁹ Simon Peter saith unto him, Lord, not my feet only, but also *my* hands and *my* head. ¹⁰ Jesus saith to him, He that is washed needeth not save to wash *his* feet, but is clean every whit: and ye are clean, but not all. ¹¹ For he knew who should betray him; therefore said he, Ye are not all clean. ¹² So after he had washed their feet, and had taken his garments, and was set down again, he said unto them, Know ye what I have done to you? ¹³ Ye call me Master and Lord: and ye say well; for *so* I am. ¹⁴ If I then, *your* Lord and Master, have washed your feet; ye also ought to wash one another's feet. ¹⁵ For I have given you an example, that ye should do as I have done to you. ¹⁶ Verily, verily, I say unto you, The servant is not greater than his lord; neither he that is sent greater than he that sent him. ¹⁷ If ye know these things, happy are ye if ye do them" (John 13:4-17).

After Jesus washed the disciples' feet, He asked them, "Know ye what I have done to you?" He answers His question in verse fourteen, "If I then, *your* Lord and Master, have washed your feet; ye also ought to wash one another's feet." Those in authority delegated foot washing to the lowest of the servants (like toilet bowl washing today). In His example of being a servant, Christ first considered the need, then considered the people, and then did what was necessary to meet the need Himself. (*Jesus washing the disciples' feet was an insignificant example of both humiliation and consideration when compared to His already great sacrifice in becoming a man.*)

The fifth and sixth characteristics of a servant's heart go hand in hand. They are hope and trust (Ruth 2:2, "I shall find grace"). Notice, there is no doubt exhibited in these words. Hope directly relates to faith. The person with faith (trust) is willing to put his life into the hands of God.

A good example is a small child jumping from the top of the stairs into his father's outstretched arms. It is his faith in his father's love and protection that leaps without hesitation. The boy attaches his body to his faith.

When we put our lives into the hands of the Lord, we can be confident He will fulfill His promises to meet our needs. God does not break promises. The next time you walk into a difficult situation of life (which is an everyday occurrence) - make sure you are holding on to the hand of your heavenly Father. He is your willing *Protector* and *Provider*. The only time you need to be concerned is when you have let go of His hand to go chasing after something in the world. God will never ask you to do anything where He will not be right beside you helping.

> "[18] And Jesus came and spake unto them, saying, All power is given unto me in heaven and in earth. [19] Go ye therefore, and teach all nations, baptizing them in the name of the Father, and of the Son, and of the Holy Ghost: [20] Teaching them to observe all things whatsoever I have commanded you: and, lo, I am with you alway, *even* unto the end of the world. Amen" (Matthew 28:18-20).

When God prompts you to do something that appears difficult or even impossible, just take His hand and do it.

The seventh characteristic of a servant's heart is that of peace or comfort in life. Notice the tranquility Ruth manifests. Notice the apparent peace in her soul. She has no apparent anxiety about her situation in life. She is in a strange land with strange people who she does not know and who do not know her, but she is not worried or concerned. Why was this possible? It is possible because of faith and hope? Yes, but it brings us in a full circle back to where we started. Death to self is equal to peace with God.

> "[7] Because the carnal mind {*Gr. the minding of the flesh*} *is* enmity against God: for it is not subject to the law of God, neither indeed can be. [8] So then they that are in the flesh cannot please God" (Romans 8:7-8).

I have had many professing Christians tell me they just do not have enough time to both work and serve God. Let me tell you why this problem exists in so many peoples' lives. They try to keep the sacred separated from the secular. In essence, they are *double minded*. They try to think in two directions at the same time (James 1:8).

Serving God is not something we do separately from the rest of our lives. Serving God is something we interweave into everything we do in our lives. Serving God is an attitude that meets each person and each situation in life with a servant's heart. That means every relationship as well - our children, our husband or wife, our employer, our employees, and our co-workers.

We do not need to find time to serve the Lord when we integrate every aspect of our lives into opportunities to serve, to encourage, to be a blessing, or to be a challenge. When we relegate living for Christ, serving Him and being a witness, to just portions of our time, we become *part time* Christians.

Opportunities to serve are endless. Available opportunities are not the issue. People with servant's hearts do not just look for opportunities to serve. They create opportunities to serve. In fact, their lives are endless opportunities because they have learned to cultivate servant's hearts.

Handfuls On Purpose
Studies in the Book of Ruth
Chapter Eight
Seven Character Traits of a Person with a Servant's Heart

1. List the seven characteristics of a servant's heart.
   A. Yie __ __ edness
   B. Hu __ __ lity
   C. Spiritual Am __ __ ition
   D. Con __ __ __ eration
   E. H __ __ e
   F. Tr __ __ t
   G. P __ __ ce

2. Read Leviticus 19:9-10. What did God's grace provide to such people as Naomi and Ruth?

3. What must each of us be fully emptied of before God can <u>fully</u> use us?

4. In order to be "filled" with the Holy Spirit, who must be dethroned in our life?

5. What is the central reason why so few Christians are ever really used of God?

6. How does Galatians 2:20 show the over-all character of a servant's heart?

7. Would you say Galatians 2:20 is descriptive of your life?

8. Read Matthew 20:27. If you want to be a spiritual leader and lead people to Christ, what is necessary before God can use you in that capacity?
   A. From that perspective, what priority would you give to learning to be a servant?
   B. Is that your present priority?

9. Read Ephesians 5:18-21. What is the central idea behind being "filled" with the Spirit?

10. Read Romans 6:11-13. What keeps the Holy Spirit from having total control of our lives?

11. What does pride try to fool us into thinking we will lose once we lose pride?

12. Read Proverbs 15:33. What does this verse reveal to us about the above question?

13. Read Proverbs 22:4. What is the reward of "humility and fear of the Lord"?

14. What is the biblical word for spiritual ambition?

15. In what way is spiritual ambition different then self-ambition?

16. What does true spiritual ambition do with praise when praise is misdirected towards self?

17. What is the difference between a *willingness* to do the work of the ministry and a *drive* to do the work of the ministry?

18. When you seek to serve the Lord, do you come to *work* or do you just <u>come</u> to work?

19. How would you define being *considerate* as it regards Christian service?

20. What is the only real way to teach people to be servants?
   A. Read John 13:12-14. How did the Creator of heaven and earth teach people to be servants?
   B. How could you apply this principle to your life in a visible and tangible way?

21. Read Romans 1:17. What is the principle for living detailed here?

22. Honestly, to what degree do you think you live this way?

23. What does "peace" with God provide in the believer's life?

24. How often do you worry about things or circumstances in your life?

25. Why do so many professing Christians say they do not have enough time to serve the Lord?

26. Establish what you need to do to integrate every moment of your life into the service of others.

Remember, every plan begins with a decision to begin, but a decision to begin is not a beginning until you begin to work your plan. The key word is *work*. A plan is just a plan until the *work* begins.

Handfuls On Purpose
Studies in the Book of Ruth
Chapter Nine
Understanding the Value of Holiness and Commitment in Realizing the Will of God for Our Lives

"[1] And Naomi had a kinsman of her husband's, a mighty man of wealth, of the family of Elimelech; and his name *was* Boaz. [2] And Ruth the Moabitess said unto Naomi, Let me now go to the field, and glean ears of corn after *him* in whose sight I shall find grace. And she said unto her, Go, my daughter. [3] And she went, and came, and gleaned in the field after the reapers: and her hap was to light on a part of the field *belonging* unto Boaz, who *was* of the kindred of Elimelech" (Ruth 2:1-3).

In our last few studies in Ruth, we saw that the full surrender of our lives to Jesus Christ is what opens the door to power with God. We saw Ruth's six resolutions of commitment. We saw the necessity of escaping the *blinders of time* to see the *blessings of eternity*. In the last lesson, we saw seven characteristics of a servant's heart. In this lesson, we want to see the confidence that belongs to the person who is totally committed to the Lord Jesus as well as to a life of obedience and holiness.

In Ruth 2:3, the Word of God informs us that it was Ruth's "hap . . . to light on a part of the field *belonging* unto Boaz." The word "hap" is from the Hebrew word *miqreh* (mik-reh'). The word means *by chance, accident,* or *fate*. Certainly, from a human perspective that is what happened. However, that is not what happened in the foreknowledge of God. God knew exactly where Ruth would end up because Ruth had put her life into God's hands to guide her every step.

"[23] The steps of a *good* man are ordered by the LORD: and he delighteth in his way. [24] Though he fall, he shall not be utterly cast down: for the LORD upholdeth *him with* his hand" (Psalm 37:23-24).

Over the years, many people have asked how they can know with certainty what God's will was for some particular area of their life. What they were really asking for was a *Jonah-like* message from God. They wanted God to speak to them and say, "Arise and go to Nineveh." Before they were willing to go, they wanted a map to appear in the sky telling them how to get there with a blueprint detailing what to do. Although God has worked that way in the past, He seldom does. Throughout all recorded history, there are only a handful of such instances. In the majority of people's lives, God has not worked that way.

It is amazing how many professing Christians believe in such things as *luck* or *fate*. What they really are saying is that they are willing to leave their lives up to *chance*. They live by the slogan, "I'll take my chances." In this lesson, we will lay the groundwork for taking *chance* out of our lives and putting our lives into the hands of God and His directing power.

There are two foundational principles that are prerequisite to *realizing* the will of God in a person's life. Notice I did not say *know* the will of God for a person's life. This chapter is not about *knowing* the will of God (other than knowing the Word of God and obeying it). This is about *realizing* God's will in our lives.

At this point in Ruth's life, do you suppose she knew she would be in the lineage of the generations of the Messiah of Israel? I doubt if she even considered the matter. Her thoughts were probably preoccupied with such things as what she would eat and how she would survive. She was thinking about the very basic issues of life like daily bread. Yet, Ruth had already established two foundational principles that would guide her footsteps to the field of Boaz and bless her life.

Foundational Principle of Faith: "The just shall live by faith." This is a principle regularly repeated in the Word of God.

"[2] And the LORD answered me, and said, Write the vision, and make *it* plain upon tables, that he may run that readeth it. [3] For the vision *is* yet for an appointed time, but at the end it shall speak, and not lie: though it tarry, wait for it; because it will surely come, it will not tarry. [4] Behold, his soul *which* is lifted up is not upright in him: but the just shall live by his faith" (Habakkuk 2:2-4).

"[16] For I am not ashamed of the gospel of Christ: for it is the power of God unto salvation to every one that believeth; to the Jew first, and also to the Greek. [17] For therein is the righteousness of God revealed from faith to faith: as it is written, The just shall live by faith" (Romans 1:16-17).

"¹⁰ For as many as are of the works of the law are under the curse: for it is written, Cursed *is* every one that continueth not in all things which are written in the book of the law to do them. ¹¹ But that no man is justified by the law in the sight of God, *it is* evident: for, The just shall live by faith" (Galatians 3:10-11).

"³⁵ Cast not away therefore your confidence, which hath great recompence of reward. ³⁶ For ye have need of patience, that, after ye have done the will of God, ye might receive the promise. ³⁷ For yet a little while, and he that shall come will come, and will not tarry. ³⁸ Now the just shall live by faith: but if *any man* draw back, my soul shall have no pleasure in him. ³⁹ But we are not of them who draw back unto perdition; but of them that believe to the saving of the soul" (Hebrews 10:35-39).

Living by faith is one of God's governing principles for life ("shall live"). However, what is the practical expression of this principle? First, it is only for the "just." Who are the "just"? "Just" is a term that refers to all those who have been justified or declared righteous because they trusted in the finished work of Christ for their salvation.

"The just" are the by-products of the satisfaction of God's justice through the substitutionary death of Jesus Christ when He paid the death sentence put upon all of mankind at the fall of Adam (Romans 5:12 and 6:23). The word "just" is also a word that implies that the one justified is committed to observing the moral Laws of God (not to be saved, but because he is saved).

Therefore, this verse says that the person who is justified by a gift of God's grace through faith in the finished and substitutionary work of Christ on behalf of all mankind (I John 2:2) "shall live by" the *principle of faith*. What does God mean by "living by faith"? For some people that means living in a Volkswagen bus waiting for their needs to fall out of the sky. That is a good example of what living by faith *does not* mean.

The word "faith" in Habakkuk 2:4 (from which all the New Testament verses are quoted) is from the Hebrew word *'emuwnah* (em-oo-naw'). It means firmness, fidelity, steadfastness or steadiness. Therefore, all of these verses are saying that the saved person ("the just") is obligated to live a life of steadfast fidelity to the Word of God and the God of the Word. When that is the reality of a person's life, that person can live with the confidence that God with direct his steps.

Another thing that is amazing about Christians is how many profess to believe in Christ, read His Word, but still seem unwilling to trust their lives into His care. They are just not willing to completely yield and obey His Word. *Doing* is a very large part of what faith is all about. Faith implies we trust God's Word enough to obey it and put its truths into practice. That is what Ruth meant in Ruth 1:16 when she committed herself by saying, "Thy God shall be my God." God is not our God until we trust Him enough with our lives to obey His Word. Any reservation in this area is not living by faith. God cannot really bless our lives until we commit to live in obedience to Him and His Word.

> "³ Who shall ascend into the hill of the LORD? or who shall stand in his holy place? ⁴ He that hath clean hands, and a pure heart; who hath not lifted up his soul unto vanity, nor sworn deceitfully. ⁵ He shall receive the blessing from the LORD, and righteousness from the God of his salvation" (Psalm 24:3-5).

The person who loves the Lord strives to live in continual fellowship with Him. That means a life of continual self examination for sin, a desire to live separated from the world and unto God (holiness), and a desire to live in obedience to God's Word. That person takes *chance* out of his life (which leads us to another foundational principle).

> "And we know that all things work together for good to them that love God, to them who are the called according to *his* purpose" (Romans 8:28).

In this verse, God's gives two qualifying requirements before "all things work together for good." First, we must understand what "all things" working "together" means. "All things" is a collective term that means we enter into a partnership with God and become an integral part of His plan and program, functioning *within* it (not in opposition to it). This is why the Word of God says, "What fellowship {*co-operative partnership*} hath righteousness with unrighteousness? And what communion {*common co-operation*} hath light with darkness" (II Corinthians 6:14)?

The point is this, when we do not separate ourselves from anything and everything in the world that is sinful, we are not functioning *within* the plan and program of God. Instead, we are living in opposition to God's plan and program.

> "[15] Love not the world, neither the things *that are* in the world. If any man love the world, the love of the Father is not in him. [16] For all that *is* in the world, the lust of the flesh, and the lust of the eyes, and the pride of life, is not of the Father, but is of the world. [17] And the world passeth away, and the lust thereof: but he that doeth the will of God abideth for ever. [18] Little children, it is the last time: and as ye have heard that antichrist shall come, even now are there many antichrists; whereby we know that it is the last time. [19] They went out from us, but they were not of us; for if they had been of us, they would *no doubt* have continued with us: but *they went out*, that they might be made manifest that they were not all of us" (I John 2:15-19).

Anytime we unite ourselves with the world in anyway, we become a part of the "all things" that are in opposition to the plan and program of God. This is what God refers to as *spiritual adultery*.

> "[3] Ye ask, and receive not, because ye ask amiss, that ye may consume *it* upon your lusts. [4] Ye adulterers and adulteresses, know ye not that the friendship of the world is enmity with God? whosoever therefore will be a friend of the world is the enemy of God" (James 4:3-4).

When we want to be part of the "all things that work together for good," doing so requires the two qualifying statements in Romans 8:28. The first qualifying statement is that we must learn to love God. Love is not some ambiguous emotion. It is an action word defined by concrete realities. God says if we love Him, we will obey Him and obedience will not be a burden to us.

> "[2] By this we know that we love the children of God, when we love God, and keep his commandments. [3] For this is the love of God, that we keep his commandments: and his commandments are not grievous" (I John 5:2-3).

The second qualifying statement is that we must put God's purpose first as a governing principle in life. We must constantly be considering what God wants in any given moment of our lives. This is an attitude of life that considers God's purpose and priorities before anything else.

When a person adopts this attitude, what happens to him in his life becomes secondary to God's purpose. Only when we love God by obedience and when God's purpose is our main priority will all things work together for good. Only then will we become part of God's collective plan for good (rather than living in opposition to it).

From the perspective of this lesson, turn to Psalm twenty-three and read it. God gives this Psalm especially for the person we have detailed in this lesson. As we all know, Psalm twenty-three is the Shepherd Psalm. The Shepherd is the One in charge of the "all things working together for good" of which we become part when we commit ourselves to obedience to God's Word (loving God) and putting God's purpose first in our decisions. The Shepherd Psalm is a Psalm of confidence in being right with God and living in His will. It is not for the wandering sheep, but for the faithful sheep.

"[1] A Psalm of David. The LORD *is* my shepherd; I shall not want. [2] He maketh me to lie down in **green** pastures {*pastures of tender grass*}: he leadeth me beside the **still** waters. {*waters of quietness*} [3] He restoreth my soul: he leadeth me in the paths of righteousness for his name's sake. [4] Yea, though I walk through the valley of the shadow of death, I will fear no evil: for thou *art* with me; thy rod and thy staff they comfort me. [5] Thou preparest a table before me in the presence of mine enemies: thou anointest my head with oil; my cup runneth over. [6] Surely goodness and mercy shall follow me all the days of my life: and I will dwell in the house of the LORD for ever" (Psalm 23:1-6).

For as long as the Christian remains within the circle of the Shepherd's care ("walk in the Light", I John 1:7), he can be confident that whatever He does will be within the Lord's will. When the believer is living in God's will by being obedient to the Word of God and putting God's purpose first in every decision he makes, God will direct his steps. So many professing Christians live in open rebellion and spiritual adultery against God and still expect

His protective custody upon their lives. That is a promise only for those that "walk in the light."

"[1] My son, forget not my law; but let thine heart keep my commandments: [2] For length of days, and long life, and peace, shall they add to thee. [3] Let not mercy and truth forsake thee: bind them about thy neck; write them upon the table of thine heart: [4] So shalt thou find favour and good understanding in the sight of God and man. [5] Trust in the LORD with all thine heart; and lean not unto thine own understanding. [6] In all thy ways acknowledge him, and he shall direct thy paths" (Proverbs 3:1-6).

Within God's will, the individual walking in the "light" (living in the center of God's truth and will) can step out in any direction and be confident his footsteps will fall right in the middle of God's will. He has three hundred and sixty degrees of choices.

"[105] Thy word *is* a lamp unto my feet, and a light unto my path. [106] I have sworn, and I will perform *it*, that I will keep thy righteous judgments" (Psalm 119:105-106).

Handfuls On Purpose
Studies in the Book of Ruth
Chapter Nine
Understanding the Value of Holiness and Commitment in Realizing the Will of God for Our Lives

1. In Ruth 2:3, what does the word "hap" mean?

2. Do you think that God wants us to leave our lives up to *chance*?

3. What does it mean to wait for a *Jonah message* from God?

4. Do you think the way in which God revealed what He wanted to Jonah is the way in which God works in everyday situations of life, or was that a special event with special circumstances?

5. What are people really saying when they say everything is just a matter of *fate*?

6. What is the difference between *fate* and the sovereign plan and purpose of God?

7. What is the difference between *knowing* the will of God for our lives and *realizing* the will of God *in* our lives?

8. From the following verses of Scripture, list the two foundational principles that are essential to realizing the will (plan) of God for your life.
   A. Romans 1:17:
   B. Romans 8:28:

9. According to Romans 1:17, to whom is this principle directed?

10. How can a person become one of these people?

11. Define in concrete and tangible terms what it means to "live by faith."

12. What does it not mean?

13. What is the action word that best describes the idea of faith?

14. What are the ramifications of Ruth's statement in Ruth 1:16, "Thy God shall be my God"?

15. Define what God means in Romans 8:28 by the term "all things."

16. How does your answer to the above question relate to the difference between functioning within God's sovereign plan or opposing that plan?

17. There are two *collectives*: the "all things that work together for good" and the *all things that work together for evil.* From II Corinthians 6:14, what is God's warning and instruction about these two *collectives*?

18. Read I John 2:15-19. When God says that certain individuals "go out from us," which *Collective* have they abandoned and which have they joined?

19. List the two qualifying statements of Romans 8:28.

20. Read I John 5:2-3. What is the concrete way in which God measures the reality of our love for Him?

21. What does it mean that God's purpose must be the priority of our life?

22. Read Psalm 23. From the context of what we have learned in this study, what is the real meaning behind the Shepherd Psalm?

23. What are you willing to do (and be) in order to have the confidence of knowing you are a part of God's wonderful and sovereign plan of the ages rather than living in opposition to that plan?

Handfuls On Purpose
Studies in the Book of Ruth
Chapter Ten
Finding the Treasure of Grace

"[1] And Naomi had a kinsman of her husband's, a mighty man of wealth, of the family of Elimelech; and his name *was* Boaz. [2] And Ruth the Moabitess said unto Naomi, Let me now go to the field, and glean ears of corn after *him* in whose sight I shall find grace. And she said unto her, Go, my daughter. [3] And she went, and came, and gleaned in the field after the reapers: and her hap was to light on a part of the field *belonging* unto Boaz, who *was* of the kindred of Elimelech" (Ruth 2:1-3).

Faith is the foundation of our relationship with the Lord (Hebrews 11:6). Faith gives us eyes to see the invisible and ears to hear the still small voice of God. Faith sees the potential of miracles in every impossible situation of life. Faith enters the *God factor* into every equation that appears to equal failure.

Have you ever watched someone with a metal detector search for *buried treasures*? He will completely cover an area of ground, back and forth, back and forth. Then suddenly a beeper begins to sound and he gets all excited. There is the potential for discovery. However, as he digs in the ground, his countenance falls when he finds his discovery is nothing but a rusty nail or a corroded tin can.

Many times a Christian's search for God's blessings ends up the same way. They are looking for *materialistic treasures.* God's blessings are spiritual and eternal. A Christian does not need to search for them like buried treasure. God's blessings find us. The priority is that we will focus on what we need to be in order for God to enable us to find His grace. The Christian's search should be for the *face of God.*

Ruth has already committed herself to the God of Israel (consecration). God has already saved her by grace through faith (therefore, this lesson is not about being saved). We want to look at what God's Word says defining what is necessary for God to bless a Christian. Ruth is prepared and willing to accept whatever lot in life God gives her. There is no implication that Ruth expected a life of ease or material wealth just because she became a believer (in fact, the opposite may be true).

The continual testimony of Scripture and history is that great people of God never expect God to remove them *from* difficulties in life. However, they do expect (and trusted in fact that) the Lord will be *with* them through their difficulty. The Lord was with His faithful servants in the fiery furnace.

> "[23] And these three men, Shadrach, Meshach, and Abednego, fell down bound into the midst of the burning fiery furnace. [24] Then Nebuchadnezzar the king was astonied, and rose up in haste, *and* spake, and said unto his counsellors, Did not we cast three men bound into the midst of the fire? They answered and said unto the king, True, O king. [25] He answered and said, Lo, I see four men loose, walking in the midst of the fire, and they have no hurt; and the form of the fourth is like the Son of God" (Daniel 3:23-25).

God's *fellowship presence* promises blessings for the faithful believer. Every believer living in fellowship with God will be living in the blessings of God. Therefore, the believer should not be seeking blessings, but fellowship with God. In that fellowship, he will find God's blessings (I John 1:7).

Ruth 2:1-3 reveals three expectations Ruth had based upon the Word of God.

1. She expected to find her Kinsman Redeemer.
2. She expected to claim her right to glean.
3. She expected to find grace (unmerited favor) in the sight of her Kinsman Redeemer.

Even though Ruth had a right to each of these expectations by God's Law, notice her attitudes of diligence, submission, humility, and appreciation.

> "[7] And she said, I pray you, let me glean and gather after the reapers among the sheaves: so she came, and hath continued even from the morning until now, that she tarried a little in the house. . . [10] Then she fell on her face, and bowed herself to the ground, and said unto him, Why have I found grace in thine eyes, that thou shouldest take knowledge of me, seeing I *am* a stranger" (Ruth 2:7 and 10)?

Ruth came claiming the promises of God and expecting to find His grace. However, grace was the real treasure Ruth sought. She sought the grace of God in the promises of God. All of God's promises are of His grace. God's promises are gifts of His love that we do not deserve. Our right to God's promises is based solely upon of the gift of His grace.

First, we must understand that God's blessings are always of grace. We can never truthfully say that we have earned or deserve God's blessings. God's blessings flow like a river to the obedient believer standing in the place of obedience. Move out of that place of loving obedience and the rivers of God's blessings will flow right past you without even touching your life. Only the obedient believer has any right to be optimistic about the blessings of God. Obedience out of love for God is the central aspect of fellowship with God.

> "But if we walk in the light, as he is in the light, we have fellowship one with another, and the blood of Jesus Christ his Son cleanseth us from all sin" (I John 1:7, "light" is a metaphor for truth and the will of God).

Secondly, we must understand that the Word of God states repeatedly that the foundation for His blessings is faith. To most people the meaning of the word faith is almost completely lost. The Bible defines the word faith.

> "^{1} Let us therefore fear, lest, a promise being left *us* of entering into his rest, any of you should seem to come short of it. ^{2} For unto us was the gospel preached, as well as unto them: but the word preached did not profit them, not being mixed with faith in them that heard *it*" (Hebrews 4:1-2).

The word "rest" (Greek: *katapausis,* kat-ap'-ow-sis) is a word that represents the whole realm of heavenly blessedness in which God dwells. Hebrews 4:2 tells us we enter <u>into</u> that realm of heavenly blessedness <u>through</u> faith.

We know from 1 Thessalonians 5:23 that man is a trichotomous being (body, soul, and spirit). Faith involves all three aspects of man's being in response to God and His Word. To understand how each of these three aspects of man is involved in response to God's word we need to use common terms with which we are acqainted. The soul is man's *psyche* (mind or intellect). The spirit is man's *emotions* or *attitudes* (the Bible calls it *heart*). The body refers to a man's *actions in life*. Therefore, when a person brings all three aspects of his being into proper alignment (submission) with God's will, because he trusts God's will for his life, that is what the Bible defines as faith. We might write a formula for this as follows:

Understanding + Attitude & Action + Submission to God's Will = Faith

The meaning of faith must involve all three components before it is biblical faith. There must be a correct understanding of God's Word. There must be correct attitudes towards God's Word (submission, humility, etc.). There must be a desire to obey God's Word. Obedience is not an attitude. Obedience is an action. The following portions of Scripture show all three aspects of faith expressed:

> "[21] Who by him do believe in God, that raised him up from the dead, and gave him glory; that your faith and hope might be in God. [22] Seeing ye have purified your souls in obeying the truth through the Spirit unto unfeigned love of the brethren, *see that ye* love one another with a pure heart fervently: [23] Being born again, not of corruptible seed, but of incorruptible, by the word of God, which liveth and abideth for ever" (I Peter 1:21-23).

> "[16] Hereby perceive we the love *of God*, because he laid down his life for us: and we ought to lay down *our* lives for the brethren. [17] But whoso hath this world's good, and seeth his brother have need, and shutteth up his bowels *of compassion* from him, how dwelleth the love of God in him? [18] My little children, let us not love in word, neither in tongue; but in deed and in truth" (I John 3:16-18).

Why could Ruth be confident of God's blessing? Why could she be so optimistic? She could be optimistic because she was a person of faith. What does it mean to be a person of faith? She understood what God wanted her to do. She had a submissive and humble spirit to His will. She was obedient and willing to work. In short, she was right with God. From this perspective read Hebrews 4:16. God gives this text to those who have entered into His rest through faith.

"Let us therefore come boldly unto the throne of grace, that we may obtain mercy, and find grace to help in time of need" (Hebrews 4:16).

When God encourages His children (those born again of the Spirit) to come "boldly unto the throne of grace," He means to come to Him with confidence that He will give His children the grace they need (as much and as often as they need it). Being right with God is what gives the believer the confidence of finding God's blessings (living by faith because of the right understanding of God's Word + right attitude towards God's Word + the willingness to be obedient to God's Word = living by faith).

God's "rest" is the realm of His blessedness. A walk in faith does not bring *it* to *you*. A walk of faith takes *you* to *it*. Blessedness is not a *thing*. Blessedness is a *place*. Most Christians do not understand this concept of spiritual blessings.

It is like the Lord taking one of His children into His *treasure chamber* and the Christian saying to the Lord, "Can I have one of these treasures? Can I have a blessing? Then, the Lord answers back, "My child, you don't understand. They are all yours. Take whatever you need." The Christian who really understands the true blessings of grace is he who understands that God's greatest blessings are not silver or gold, but living in the intimacy of His presence.

Is there a big empty hole in your life? Does it seem sometimes like you stand outside of your life without any real control of what happens? Do you find yourself dreading another tomorrow? The problem is that you are focusing on finding blessings in your life. Start focusing on the *Blessor* (God) and your relationship with Him. Then the fog will lift and the blessings already in your life will become visible.

When God says "The just shall live by faith," He is talking about a faith relationship with Him. You do your part (right understanding + right attitude + obedience = a faith relationship) and God will do His part. You are living in God's treasure room of grace, but only true faith will be able to see what is available to you at your fingertips. **The treasure is God!**

Handfuls On Purpose
Studies in the Book of Ruth
Chapter Ten
Finding the Treasure of Grace

1. Discuss the importance of faith to our relationship with the Lord.

2. How do most people define the blessings of God?

3. Do you think Ruth was expecting a life of ease, without trials or difficulties, just because she became a believer?

4. Read Daniel 3:23-25. From this account, did Daniel expect God to remove him from the difficult trials of life? What did he expect?

5. Where God is, there will be blessings. If that statement is true and you want to be blessed of God, where should you strive to be (I John 1:7)?

6. According to Ruth 2:1-3, Ruth had three expectations based upon her understanding of what God revealed in His Word. What were they?

7. Read Ruth 2:7, 10. Although Ruth had the right to each of these expectations by Law, what words would you use to describe her attitude?

8. Discuss the meaning of the word "grace" and how the blessings of grace can never be deserved or earned and still fall under the context of that meaning.

9. Read Hebrews 4:1-2. Discuss the meaning of the word "rest" and how this meaning relates to the believer's faith in God.

10. Discuss the trichotomy of man and how each aspect of man's being is involved in defining faith.

11. Discuss why Ruth could be confident of God's blessing and optimistic.

12. Discuss the following statements: God's "rest" is the realm of His blessedness. A walk in faith does not bring it to you. A walk of faith takes you to it. Blessedness is not a *thing*. Blessedness is a *place*.

13. What is the real blessing (treasure) of grace?

Handfuls On Purpose
Studies in the Book of Ruth
Chapter Eleven
Boaz as a Type of Christ

"[4] And, behold, Boaz came from Bethlehem, and said unto the reapers, The LORD *be* with you. And they answered him, The LORD bless thee. [5] Then said Boaz unto his servant that was set over the reapers, Whose damsel *is* this? [6] And the servant that was set over the reapers answered and said, It *is* the Moabitish damsel that came back with Naomi out of the country of Moab: [7] And she said, I pray you, let me glean and gather after the reapers among the sheaves: so she came, and hath continued even from the morning until now, that she tarried a little in the house. [8] Then said Boaz unto Ruth, Hearest thou not, my daughter? Go not to glean in another field, neither go from hence, but abide here fast by my maidens: [9] *Let* thine eyes *be* on the field that they do reap, and go thou after them: have I not charged the young men that they shall not touch thee? and when thou art athirst, go unto the vessels, and drink of *that* which the young men have drawn" (Ruth 2:4-9).

In this text, we see Boaz as a type of Christ. We see him from two different perspectives. We see him as lord over his servants, but yet in a working relationship with those servants. We see him in the beginnings of his relationship with Ruth. Here we see him as a man of generosity, compassion, tenderness, and sacrificial love as he seeks to bring Ruth to spiritual maturity. These ideas should be in our minds as we think of our relationship with Christ.

Parents, have you ever stopped to ask yourselves what goes through your child's mind at the mention of your name? Have you ever thought how your child's perspective of you as a father or mother changes as he grows up and how he begins to see you differently in different stages of his maturing process?

Children begin to formulate opinions of their parents very early in their lives based upon how we interact with them and respond to what they do. Their opinions of their parents develop through their experiences in how we meet their needs, how we discipline them when they disobey, and encourage them when they obey. Children go through a number of stages as they grow to maturity.

1. The stage of *infancy* and *innocence* (about one week long)
2. The stage of *stumbling* (the terrible twos)
3. The stage of *bumbling* (3-7)
4. The stage of *mumbling* (8-12)
5. The stage of *grumbling* (teens)
6. The stage of *rambling* (young adulthood)
7. The stage of *maturity* (adulthood - sometimes never achieved)

In the Bible, there are seven distinct time-periods called *Dispensations* in which God tests man's obedience to His will. When we take an overall view of these Dispensations of God, it is as if we are watching God's creation grow from infancy to adulthood in human responsibility and in its relationship to its Creator.

In the Garden of Eden, humanity is like an innocent baby. When they sinned, they had their first taste of both God's love and grace. Immediately after that, they got their first taste of God's disciplinary action upon their sin. We learn early in the development of the fall of humanity that because of sin, man *grows away* from God not *towards* Him. God's disciplinary action is intent on correcting that movement (negative growth) away from Him. All of this affected how individuals view God and the continuing development of their perspective of Him over the years of their lives. When discipline failed to correct that perspective, they distorted their knowledge of God proportionately and their rebellion became more apparent.

Therefore, as we move historically through Scripture, we see man increasingly distorting and perverting his perspective of God. We see a loving, compassionate God continuing to do whatever is necessary to move man back to growth towards Him (spiritual maturity). Sometimes this required some very harsh actions (like the flood). Yet, with each new Dispensation, God would begin again with new representative people who had been restored to the place of spiritual maturity. This remnant was the people who corrected their understanding of who God is. Then they are given the responsibility to go forth and "replenish the earth" (Genesis 1:28) with the responsibility of teaching the next generation about who God is and about His expectations of them. The history of the world is a history of failure in this simple responsibility.

In the Genesis creation, humanity sees God from the perspective of awe, bigger than life, as a child (an infant) must see his parents, yet with little comprehension of what he sees. Therefore, immediately a child begins to take his parents for granted.

A child develops his perspective of his parents. He develops his perspective from the opinions he formulates about them in the way his parents interact with him. He develops his perspective in the way his parents relate to him through love, meeting needs, discipline, and character molding. Yet, when children become adults, they seldom look back to re-evaluate the process of the childhood development that made them. Instead, we presuppose our character is what it ought to be because we learned character by experience and because we are what we are.

As a teenager, my father seem hard, perhaps even cruel. From that perspective, his whole purpose in life seemed intent on eliminating anything enjoyment. As an adult, I understood he was simply trying to protect me from my impulsive, quick-tempered *self,* when at a time in my life any one mistake might affect me for the rest of my life.

Looking back on the same man, once viewed as hard and unloving, it became obvious that he was a man of tenderness, genuine love (not the emotional kind), and continuing grace. Why grace? Because even though I was fighting him all the way, he never quit being my dad. Even though I resisted him at every turn, he loved me enough to keep at it.

This is what God does in bringing us to spiritual maturity. Yet God goes far beyond that. His love goes to extremes to which no man could ever go, or even imagine. This is what grace is all about. This is what defines the God of all grace. Sadly, most Christians do not see the God of all grace until they come to spiritual maturity. Until then, we lock our perspective of God into whatever level of spiritual growth in which we are presently exist. Until we can understand what we deserve compared to what He has given, we will never really appreciate who God is. Only then, will we understand what the word *grace* means. Then we will understand the God of all grace.

How many Christians read John 3:16 and see only the benefits to themselves? How many of us really stop to think about the God who "so loved the world He gave"? He did not give because we deserved His gift. He gave because He loves us. Boaz typifies the God of love and grace. God separates these aspects of

His character from other aspects of His character. God wants these aspects of His character standing apart so that we might see His workings flowing from His nature rather than from our need.

Those who knew Boaz loved and respected him (Ruth 2:4). This knowledge and respect of Boaz came from years of working with him and the intimate knowledge of his character that came from that relationship. These reapers represent mature believers. There is mutual respect because of Boaz's consistency in his dealings with these people. There is also a degree of intimacy implied in Ruth 2:4 between these men and Boaz. They not only harvested together, but also fought together.

The central reason this kind of relationship between Boaz and these men existed was because Boaz was more than just a lord over the work. He was a *partner* with them in the work.

> "[35] And Jesus went about all the cities and villages, teaching in their synagogues, and preaching the gospel of the kingdom, and healing every sickness and every disease among the people. [36] But when he saw the multitudes, he was moved with compassion on them, because they fainted, and were scattered abroad, as sheep having no shepherd. [37] Then saith he unto his disciples, The harvest truly *is* plenteous, but the labourers *are* few; [38] Pray ye therefore the Lord of the harvest, that he will send forth labourers into his harvest" (Matthew 9:35-38).

Jesus is the "Lord of the harvest" (v. 38). He is also a co-worker in the harvest (v. 35). This is the continuing promise in the Great Commission.

> "[18] And Jesus came and spake unto them, saying, All power is given unto me in heaven and in earth. [19] Go ye therefore, and **teach** all nations {*or, make disciples, or, Christians of all nations*}, baptizing them in the name of the Father, and of the Son, and of the Holy Ghost: [20] Teaching them to observe all things whatsoever I have commanded you: and, lo, I am with you alway, *even* unto the end of the world. Amen" (Matthew 28:18-20).

Although we live in the Age of Grace, we are not on *vacation*. The believer's partnership with Christ is a working partnership. Spiritually mature believers who have a relationship with God based upon knowledge and experience most effectively do the work of the ministry. That is the pattern established in Scripture.

"¹¹ And he gave some, apostles; and some, prophets; and some, evangelists; and some, pastors and teachers; ¹² For the perfecting of the saints, for the work of the ministry, for the edifying of the body of Christ: ¹³ Till we all come in the unity of the faith, and of the knowledge of the Son of God, unto a perfect man, unto the measure of the **stature** {*or age; refers to spiritual maturity*} of the fulness of Christ: ¹⁴ That we *henceforth* be no more children, tossed to and fro, and carried about with every wind of doctrine, by the sleight of men, *and* cunning craftiness, whereby they lie in wait to deceive; ¹⁵ But speaking the truth in love, may grow up into him in all things, which is the head, *even* Christ: ¹⁶ From whom the whole body fitly joined together and compacted by that which every joint supplieth, according to the effectual working in the measure of every part, maketh increase of the body unto the edifying of itself in love" (Ephesians 4:11-16).

For over one-hundred years now, the focus of evangelism has been almost exclusively *production centered* (soul winning, we call this *evangelism*). This has resulted in many professions of faith, but very few laborers for the harvest because of the failure to disciple people in the *model of ministry* (work). Although this type of *evangelism* seems noble, it has actually proven to be detrimental to the advancement of Christianity.

The context of Ephesians 4:11-16 flows from the truth of Ephesians 4:1. Every believer has a "vocation" in Christ that he is being prepared to fulfill through his local church.

"I therefore, the prisoner of the Lord, beseech you that ye walk worthy of the vocation wherewith ye are called," (Ephesians 4:1).

Yet, only mature believers are prepared to be effective ministers (workers) for Christ. Soul winning is only the first step in the "work of the ministry." The new believer must be brought to understand his need to *die to self* and *live in the resurrection power of Jesus Christ*. That is why water baptism is the next step in the Great Commission. Baptized believers are then united to a local church where they will be taught the Word of God, how to live, and how to be effective in reaching their world for Christ.

Today's Christianity has become so enamored with large crowds of people as a measurement of success, we seem grateful for people who are willing to take a few hours out of their busy schedules to come to Sunday service. Sunday services are about equipping, training, and preaching to prepare and motivate believers to do the "work of the ministry." Christians do the vast majority of the "work of the ministry" outside the church assembly in the world. We accomplish our greatest spiritual growth by doing the work of the ministry alongside of someone who is spiritually mature.

God expects mature believers to be involved in doing the "work of the ministry." God defines the "work of the ministry" as preaching the Gospel, winning souls, getting them baptized and into a local church where they can be taught the truths of God, how to live for Christ, and how to continue the cycle of reproducing disciples for Jesus Christ.

> "^{28} Come unto me, all *ye* that labour and are heavy laden, and I will give you rest. ^{29} Take my yoke upon you, and learn of me; for I am meek and lowly in heart: and ye shall find rest unto your souls. ^{30} For my yoke *is* easy, and my burden is light" (Matthew 11:28-30).

This verse is not a salvation invitation. The invitation of Matthew 11:28-30 is an invitation to all believers to join Christ in partnership in the work of the ministry. The "yoke" metaphor is about a working relationship/partnership with Christ. Matthew 11:29 is a description of the Lord Jesus Christ who is the "Lord of the harvest."

This working relationship of Christ with believers is in harvesting souls and warring against satanic forces of evil, deception, and the distortions of God's character. Notice that Jesus is not a hard taskmaster who drives His partners beyond their capabilities. He joins Himself with us in the work that He has called us to do. If you are suffering from spiritual *burnout*, it is because you have been pulling in your own power. Every time the thought, "I am doing more than my share" springs into your mind, understand that you are either:

1. Getting ahead of Christ (*yokefellows* must pull together)
2. Working in the flesh (you are not in fellowship with Christ-meaning you are not *yoked* with Christ)

When we become a "yoke" fellow with Christ, *then* the yoke is easy and the burden light (learn that truth). Yes, the work requires *time* and *effort* on our part or it is not work.

The camaraderie that existed between Boaz (a type of Christ) and his laborers was not by accident. It existed because they worked and fought together. These workers were much more than mere acquaintances or employees of Boaz. They had an intimacy that came from a *working relationship*. That is the relationship available to all Christians if they are willing to join in the work with Christ.

Handfuls On Purpose
Studies in the Book of Ruth
Chapter Eleven
Boaz as a Type of Christ

1. What visual image do you get of God when you think of Him as He is portrayed in the Garden of Eden?

2. What visual image do you get of God when you think of Him as He is portrayed at Mt. Sinai after Israel crossed the Red Sea?

3. What visual image do you get of God at the mention of the Cross of Calvary and the crucifixion of the *carpenter's son*?

4. What visual image to you get when you think of Christ and the Great White Throne Judgment of Revelation 20:11-15?

5. Which of the above is the correct image of Christ?

6. How does spiritual maturity affect your understanding of the above questions and the progressive development of a biblical perspective of who God is and what He is like?

7. Describe your present perspective of who God is and what He is like.

8. Discuss the difference from your present perspective of God and what it was a number of years ago.

9. When you read John 3:16, what do you see as the focus of the verse?

10. Boaz typifies Christ as a God of love and grace in the book of Ruth. From Ruth 2:4, we can see Boaz was not just Lord over the work, but a _____ with his servants in the work.

11. Read Matthew 9:35-38. Jesus is the "Lord of the harvest." According to verse 35, what else is He?

12. What is the practical value to you of your answer to the above question?

13. Explain *Production Centered Evangelism* and why it has proven to be a failure in reaching the world for Christ.

14. Read Matthew 28:18-20. Define *Perfection Centered Evangelism* as you explain the three phases of evangelism from these verses.

15. Read Ephesians 4:1, 11-16. Discuss God's ordained method to accomplish *Perfection Centered Evangelism*.

16. What must God accomplished in the life of a believer before he is *effectively* prepared to "do the work of the ministry"?

17. Discuss the difference between worship and the "work of the ministry." Discuss how misunderstanding these two hinder God in using many people.

18. What is the fastest road to spiritual maturity?

19. Read Matthew 11:28-30. Discuss how this statement by Christ is similar to the type of Christ we see in Boaz in Ruth 2:4.

20. Define "the work of the ministry" in tangible terms.

21. According to Matthew 11:29, what is the qualification <u>before</u> the "yoke is easy and the burden light"?

22. What two things does all work require?

Handfuls On Purpose
Studies in the Book of Ruth
Chapter Twelve
The Security of God's Protection in the Center of His Will

"⁴ And, behold, Boaz came from Bethlehem, and said unto the reapers, The LORD *be* with you. And they answered him, The LORD bless thee. ⁵ Then said Boaz unto his servant that was set over the reapers, Whose damsel *is* this? ⁶ And the servant that was set over the reapers answered and said, It *is* the Moabitish damsel that came back with Naomi out of the country of Moab: ⁷ And she said, I pray you, let me glean and gather after the reapers among the sheaves: so she came, and hath continued even from the morning until now, that she tarried a little in the house. ⁸ Then said Boaz unto Ruth, Hearest thou not, my daughter? Go not to glean in another field, neither go from hence, but abide here fast by my maidens: ⁹ *Let* thine eyes *be* on the field that they do reap, and go thou after them: have I not charged the young men that they shall not touch thee? and when thou art athirst, go unto the vessels, and drink of *that* which the young men have drawn. ¹⁰ Then she fell on her face, and bowed herself to the ground, and said unto him, Why have I found grace in thine eyes, that thou shouldest take knowledge of me, seeing I *am* a stranger? ¹¹ And Boaz answered and said unto her, It hath fully been shewed me, all that thou hast done unto thy mother in law since the death of thine husband: and *how* thou hast left thy father and thy mother, and the land of thy nativity, and art come unto a people which thou knewest not heretofore. ¹² The LORD recompense thy work, and a full reward be given thee of the LORD God of Israel, under whose wings thou art come to trust" (Ruth 2:4-12).

Apparently, from the question of verse eight ("Hearest thou not, my daughter?"), Ruth had not taken the dangers of her situation seriously. Perhaps she had wandered into another field (which appears to be the case). God delivered Ruth from the extreme and perverse paganism that existed in the country of Moab. Now she lived in a land where the people professed to believe in the one true God and live for Him. Ruth was just a *spiritual infant*. She did not understand that everyone that professed faith in God did not live that faith.

Ruth was an unprotected woman. That was a very dangerous thing to be during this period of history. Without a father or husband to protect them, women lived in constant danger of others victimizing, assaulting, raping, and even kidnapping them to sell them into slavery. The Pharisees often prayed and thanked God that they were not born a Samaritan, a woman, or a dog.

Ruth lived in a society where war was a normal way of resolving problems. The Philistines frequently raided the area where she now lived, killing people, stealing harvested crops, and taking women and children as slaves. It was a dangerous period of history for everyone, especially an unprotected woman. Strength and the ability to protect one's household was an important commodity.

Ruth is a type of Gentile believers. She (like all believers) needed a *Protector*. Boaz is a type of Christ. He volunteers to be Ruth's *Protector*. Yet, according to Ruth 2:8-12, he conditions his protection of Ruth upon her obedience to his instructions. Boaz could insure Ruth's protection only within certain boundaries.

As we study this text, it is important to understand this is not a salvation application. God has already saved Ruth "by grace through faith." The application is for believers and what we must do to avoid the pitfalls that lie in wait for us outside of God's will. To understand the historical and cultural context, we need to go back to Ruth 1:9.

> "The LORD grant you that ye may find rest, each *of you* in the house of her husband. Then she kissed them; and they lifted up their voice, and wept" (Ruth 1:9).

The word "rest" is a key word to understanding the purpose of the book of Ruth and the believer's position in Jesus Christ. It is the Hebrew word *menuwchah* (men-oo-khaw'). This word simply means a *place of rest* or *security*. The text defines this *place of rest* or *security* as existing "in the house of her husband." Essentially, it refers to a *safe shelter* or *place of security and protection* as the result of the ability of a husband or father. That context of meaning continues throughout the book of Ruth.

> "Then Naomi her mother in law said unto her, My daughter, shall I not seek rest for thee, that it may be well with thee" (Ruth 3:1)?

Redemption would bring Ruth into that place of "rest"

(security and protection). It would be Boaz (a type of Christ) as he takes Ruth for his wife that is the force behind her security and protection. This is a position that all believers have in our relationship as the espoused bride of Jesus Christ.

> "The LORD *is* my rock, and my fortress, and my deliverer; my God, my strength, in whom I will trust; my buckler, and the horn of my salvation, *and* my high tower" (Psalm 18:2).

However, many Christians are like Ruth. They are either ignorant of the dangers that surround them or they are just too spiritually immature to be aware of them. Yet these dangers are there and they are real.

The believer lives in constant spiritual danger (I Peter 5:6-9). The spiritual infant's knowledge of spiritual truth and spiritual dangers is almost non-existent. These are exactly the type of individuals Satan preys upon.

> "[6] Humble yourselves therefore under the mighty hand of God, that he may exalt you in due time: [7] Casting all your care upon him; for he careth for you. [8] Be sober, be vigilant; because your adversary the devil, as a roaring lion, walketh about, seeking whom he may devour: [9] Whom resist stedfast in the faith, knowing that the same afflictions are accomplished in your brethren that are in the world" (I Peter 5:6-9).

The word "care" in I Peter 5:7 is from the Greek word *merimna* (mer'-im-nah). It refers to the things that cause us concern or worry. Concerns exist because of our weaknesses and inabilities. God has no weaknesses or inabilities. God genuinely cares for His children and wants to handle their concerns.

We must come before God in humility and honestly accept the fact that we have situations in our life with which we have absolutely no means of dealing. We must believe God can handle these situations. He wants to. That does not mean you can go through life with a careless attitude of irresponsibility. When it comes to the practical aspects of everyday living, the believer has to learn to make responsible decisions that keep him in the center of God's will. The believer has a powerful "adversary" (I Peter 5:8). He is nowhere near as powerful as God is, but he is far more powerful and cunning than the believer.

Boaz had a *security system* in place. As long as Ruth remained within the confines of the boundaries established for her, she was safe. God has a similar *security system* in place. As long as the believer remains in God's will, he is safe from the adversary. I Peter 5:8 defines the believer's responsibilities.

1. He is to be "sober." "Sober" is from the Greek word *nepho* (nay'-fo), meaning to stay calm and collected.
2. He is to be "vigilant." "Vigilant" is from the Greek word *gregoreuo* (gray-gor-yoo'-o), meaning to be extremely cautious.

The meanings of these two words reveal the constant danger in which the believer lives. If the believer does not maintain his spiritual composure ("sober") and is not extremely careful ("vigilant"), his carelessness might cause him to stumble into an inescapable situation. Satan lays *spiritual traps* everywhere. Satan will spring one of his traps when a believer is at his weakest moment.

According to I Peter 5:9, in order to remain in God's *protective custody*, the believer is required to personally participate with God. In other words "casting all your care upon" God is not a passive, non-participatory act. It is a *partnership* with God.

"Whom resist stedfast in the faith, knowing that the same afflictions are accomplished in your brethren that are in the world" (I Peter 5:9).

Christians must learn that there are protective boundaries within God's will (Ruth 2:8-9). Ruth 2:8 tells us, "Go not to glean in another field." God has exact boundaries of absolute truths for us to live in. God gives moral laws to protect us and to keep us from wandering into areas of sin that will destroy our lives and the lives of our families. There is great freedom and security within these boundaries of truth. When we step outside of those boundaries, we place ourselves in grave danger. The adversary sets his traps just outside of the boundaries of truth.

"Abide here fast by my maidens" (Ruth 2:8). Ruth (like all new believers) did not know all the boundaries. Therefore, Boaz directs her to follow those who knew the boundaries. God has ordained the local church for this purpose. A biblical local church provides a multitude of spiritually mature people able to give counsel and to be examples.

"Where no counsel *is*, the people fall: but in the multitude of counsellors *there is* safety" (Proverbs 11:14).

"Let thine eyes be on the field that they do reap and go after them" (v. 9). We need to be careful that we not only keep our bodies under control and within the boundaries of truth, but also keep our wants and desires ("eyes") within those boundaries. What we fix our eyes on will become the object of our desires.

"Have I not charged the young men that they shall not touch thee" (v. 9)? There is safety and security in God's family, because God holds all of his servants directly accountable to Him. Secondly, there is safety and security in God's family, because His children are covenant people who are committed to live together under certain moral standards and obligations.

This is why a local church is an exclusive organization requiring a believer to agree to certain beliefs and to live by certain moral standards. This is why, when a believer falls in sin, the local congregation is to put him under church discipline. It is a probationary period where that individual proves his willingness to bring his life into alignment with the beliefs and practices of a covenant people. The safety and security of every individual in a local church is at risk when one member decides to break covenant.

Ruth's response to Boaz's instructions should be the response of all Christians to God's moral laws and commands (2:10). What would have happened to Ruth had she not obeyed Boaz? Would she have benefited from the *safe shelter* of Boaz's protection if she decided to live outside of his established boundaries?

The *why* question of Ruth to Boaz is an important question of which every believer should seek an answer. Why does God "take knowledge" of us? Why should God even care? Why should God want to provide us His protection? Obviously, it is not because of who we are, but because of who God is. The answer is that God responds to the believer's faith (2:11). Ruth showed real change in her life. She joined herself to God's "people" (v. 11) and became one with them in a common faith. She accepted their laws, customs, and policies. She agreed to live by their laws, customs, and policies and put herself under them. It was evident to Boaz that she was making every effort to do so.

Far too many Christians think they can go anywhere and do anything they want while claiming independence and spiritual liberty. This is not how covenant people think or live. "Trust" (v. 12) is to obey the instructions of the one you trust. You trust your life into that person's care.

When Boaz gave Ruth the instructions of verses 8-9 for her protection and provision, I doubt very much if she complained that his instructions were too limiting and restrictive. Why did she not complain? She did not complain because she knew and understood there were real dangers outside of those fixed perimeters and she could not be protected if she wandered outside of them. We will only find God's protection and provision under His "wings" (v. 12). This means we will find God's protection and provision within His will. If we move outside of God's will, we are *on our own*.

> "[15] And when ye spread forth your hands, I will hide mine eyes from you: yea, when ye make many prayers, I will not hear: your hands are full of blood. [16] Wash you, make you clean; put away the evil of your doings from before mine eyes; cease to do evil; [17] Learn to do well; seek judgment, relieve the oppressed, judge the fatherless, plead for the widow. [18] Come now, and let us reason together, saith the LORD: though your sins be as scarlet, they shall be as white as snow; though they be red like crimson, they shall be as wool. [19] If ye be willing and obedient, ye shall eat the good of the land: [20] But if ye refuse and rebel, ye shall be devoured with the sword: for the mouth of the LORD hath spoken *it*" (Isaiah 1:15-20).

God conditions His protection and His provision on obedience (v. 19). Refusing (v. 20) God's instruction by rebelling against His will is a guarantee that the "roaring lion" of evil destruction will devour the believer. It is not that God cannot protect you when you live in sin, but that He *will not protect you*.

Handfuls On Purpose
Studies in the Book of Ruth
Chapter Twelve
The Security of God's Protection in the Center of His Will

1. What can we presume Ruth was doing by the question Boaz asks her in Ruth 2:8?

2. Discuss the political environment of Bethlehem in the days of the Judges and why Ruth would have been in constant danger.

3. What do Ruth and Boaz represent as types?

4. Discuss why it is important to understand that Ruth is already saved and the context is not about salvation but the benefits of salvation.

5. Read Ruth 1:9 and 3:1. Discuss the meaning of the word "rest" and its significance to the book of Ruth.

6. Read Psalm 18:2. Who is the force behind the provision and protection of the obedient believer?

7. Why is it that so many Christians remain unaware of the extreme dangers that exist outside of the circle of God's will?

8. Read I Peter 5:6-9. Does Satan pose any real danger to the believer who remains within the circle of God's will? If not, why not?

9. What does God mean in I Peter 5:8 when He says Satan is the believer's adversary?

10. Discuss the meaning of the word "sober" from I Peter 5:8 and its spiritual significance.

11. Discuss the meaning of the word "vigilant" from I Peter 5:8 and its spiritual significance.

12. Discuss the spiritual significance of the statement "resist steadfast in the faith," especially the difference between this being a passive act or a cooperative effort with God.

13. How would you describe the degree of intensity implied in the command of I Peter 5:9?

14. Detail the significance of the following statements from Ruth and apply them to your life.
    A. "Go not to glean in another field" (2:8).
    B. "Abide here fast by my maidens" (2:8).
    C. Compare Proverbs 11:14 to your previous answer.
    D. "Let thine eyes be on the field that they do reap and go thou after them" (2:9).
    E. "Have I not charged the young men that they shall not touch thee" (2:9)?

15. Discuss the spiritual significance of Ruth's response to Boaz's statement (2:10) and why it should be every believer's response to God's provision of protection.

16. Discuss the concept of "trust" from Ruth 2:12 and what is involved in trusting God.

17. Read Isaiah 1:15-20. Discuss the conditions of God's provision and protection from this portion of Scripture.

Handfuls On Purpose
Studies in the Book of Ruth
Chapter Thirteen
Dealing with Conflict and Problems God's Way

"The LORD recompense thy work, and a full reward be given thee of the LORD God of Israel, under whose wings thou art come to trust" (Ruth 2:12).

When we read this verse, we would not view Ruth's life as being in great conflict. Yet it was. She was not even sure if she and Naomi would have food to eat. She was just doing the best she could with the life she had. Her life was certainly not a *bed of roses*. She had to work very hard each day just to survive. Dealing with conflict is a normal part of life. God is there with us to guide us through conflict if we will let Him.

There is a difference in the Bible in being *saved* and being a Christian. All true Christians are saved people, but not all saved people are Christians. Being a Christian is defined by living under the Lordship of Christ according to the principles and precepts of His teachings. The term Christian was a word coined by Caesar's Praetorian guards because they saw that the followers of Christ were willing to die for Him, just as they were willing to die for Caesar. The difference between these two terms (being *saved* and being a *Christian*) is what defines the *Christian's conflict*.

When my son Brock was five years old, his mother and I were faced with a moment of conflict in his relationship with us. There was an occasion that warranted some discipline, as is the occasional need in most five year olds. Being a strong willed young man, he decided he no longer wanted to live under the same roof with a couple of tyrants like his dad and mom.

He marched right up and told us he was running away from home. Understanding the *prodigal principle* from the example of the father in the story of the prodigal son, we said, okay and promptly began to help him pack. My wife made him a sandwich and we packed a little suitcase with some of his clothes and toys. We made sure he knew we loved him, told him we were sorry to see him leave so early in his life, and helped him out the front door (to his amazement).

We did not know what he would do or where he would go so we watched him carefully through a crack in the drapes. For about a half hour he walked up and down the half block in front of our house, carrying that suitcase. Finally, he came knocking on the front door asking permission to come home. We welcomed him home and *killed the fatted calf* (he ate his baloney sandwich). Once back inside the house, we asked him why he never went any farther than the end of the block. To which he replied, "You know I am not allowed to go across the street."

This is a small and innocent example of how we can use conflict to both learn and teach. Even though we watched him carefully, we were concerned about him. We love him greatly. Patty stood beside me holding my arm crying as we watched him walk up and down that street. We love him, but for that short period, fellowship was broken. He needed to learn that dad and mom meant what they said. He needed to learn that his place of security and blessing was in the center of obedience. Throughout the conflict, we were always his parents and he was always our son. However, during the conflict he was not living as if he was our son.

We cannot live in rebellion against God and still consider ourselves Christians. We are not talking about salvation here. Being a Christian describes a way of life. Before the word Christian was *coined*, early believers were called *Followers of the Way*. If we live in rebellion against God Word, we may be His children, but we are not living as His children should live. In that case, we may be saved, but we are not living like a Christian.

God must view his children much the same way as Patty and I watched our little five-year-old son run away in rebellion. He was not running away from home. He was running away from authority over his life. He chose to run out from under the "wings" of security and protection, rather than live under the authority of the one who provided them.

That is the story of Ruth chapter one. The family of Elimelech and Naomi came under the chastening hand of God. Because of Israel's refusal to be separate from the heathen, God brought famine in their land. Instead of blessing, there was conflict in the House of Bread (Bethlehem). Elimelech and Naomi packed their little suitcases and ran away from home. All God wanted was confession and repentance. They departed from under His wings and left the place of His protection and security to go live in Moab with the heathen. There, they were on their own and Satan began to devour them one by one until only Naomi remained. This happened because they did not know how to (or refused to) do right.

What we want to learn from this lesson is that God uses problems and conflict to teach us and strengthen us. Satan uses conflict to lure us out from under God's wings so he can destroy our lives. Then Satan uses our pride to keep us from confessing our sin, seeking God's forgiveness, and resolving the conflict. Naomi had to eat the bitter meal of her own pride before she could get right with God (1:20).

It is obvious that Ruth is in a very difficult situation. She is a new believer in a strange land, living by the ancient means of public support - gleaning. She is at the mercy of the grace of others. At this point in her life, she is usually in constant danger. Her problems are serious and her life holds enormous conflict. However, in this text she seems almost oblivious to those circumstances. Unlike Elimelech and Naomi in chapter one, Ruth has determined to remain "under the wings" of the God of Israel in whom she had come to trust (2:12).

How we handle conflict and problems is a great measurement of the reality of our faith. This reality is best measured by conflict. We can learn some excellent lessons from Ruth as she lives with the difficulty of her life situation and circumstances. Through these difficulties, she sees how God works in her life as she translates what little she knows of the Word of God into the language of a living faith.

It is only as she remains obedient to God in what she knows that God is able to offer her the sheltering protection of His "wings." She could easily have gone back to the wealth, safety, and security of her father's house in Moab, but she would not. She was like the Psalmist who said:

> "I had rather be a doorkeeper in the house of my God, than to dwell in the tents of wickedness. For the LORD God is a sun and shield: the LORD will give grace and glory: no good thing will He withhold from them that walk uprightly. 0 LORD of hosts, blessed is the man that trusteth in thee" (Psalm 84:10-12).

The arena of personal conflict is always a battlefield upon which God tests the reality of our faith. There, He wages war with the forces of evil to help us advance in *baby-steps* of growth. Unless we understand what God is doing, we may end up viewing that conflict from a very selfish perspective and actually join hands with the forces of evil, move out from under God's wings of sheltering protection, and begin to oppose ourselves. That is how God describes the unrepentant and disobedient in His Word.

> "And the servant of the Lord must not strive; but be gentle unto all men, apt to teach, patient, in meekness instructing <u>those</u> <u>that</u> <u>oppose</u> <u>themselves</u> if God peradventure will give them repentance to the acknowledging of the truth; and that they may recover themselves out of the snare of the devil, who are taken captive by him at his will" (II Timothy 2:24-26).

Because many people do not understand what God is doing in conflict, it is like watching a mother trying to wash the face of her toddler. Each time she tries to get to the area that needs cleaning the child jerks his head away. Sometimes it becomes quite a drawn out battle ending with the child in tears.

Under conflict, God is trying to *clean our faces* of things like pride, arrogance, anger, unforgiveness, hatred, and a hundred other motivational forces of our sinful natures. When the "washing of water by the Word" (Ephesians 5:26) comes upon the dirty faces of our sinful practices, we need to learn to stand still and lift our faces to God, allowing Him to remove from our lives those things that our failure in conflict exposes. Mothers do not like their children to have dirty faces because it reflects on their care for them. You can be sure God cares for His children enough to do whatever is necessary to make sure our lives are clean!

The central objective of this study is to understand God's purpose in conflict. The secondary objective is to take away the tools of deception that Satan uses in conflict to lure believers out from under God's wings of security and protection.

> "[17] Now in this that I declare *unto you* I praise *you* not, that ye come together not for the better, but for the worse. [18] For first of all, when ye come together in the church, I hear that there be divisions among you; and I partly believe it. [19] For there must be also heresies among

you, that they which are approved may be made manifest among you" (I Corinthians 11:17-19).

The word "heresies" is from the Greek word *hairesis* (hah'-ee-res-is), which refers to dissensions arising from diversity of opinions. Notice God says "there must be heresies among you." Why *must* there be heresies? When we learn why, we can use this to disarm Satan from using conflict against us.

In every relationship there is eventually going to be dissention because of a difference of opinion. Expect it. How we view that conflict will determine whether Satan will be able to use the conflict against us and destroy that relationship.

Remember, God wants to use conflict to aid in our spiritual growth. Satan wants to use conflict to hinder our spiritual growth. If we want God habitually to use conflict to benefit us, we must learn to view conflict positively, not negatively.

> "² My brethren, count it all joy when ye fall into divers temptations {*trials*}; ³ Knowing *this*, that the trying of your faith worketh patience. ⁴ But let patience have *her* perfect work, that ye may be perfect and entire, wanting nothing" (James 1:2-4).

When we learn to view conflict as an opportunity for spiritual growth rather than something we avoid at any costs, we will learn to use it to teach and to observe.

According to I Corinthians 11:19, dissentions must exist "that" (in order that) "they which are approved may be manifest among you." The word "approved" is from the Greek word *dokimos* (dok'-ee-mos). Understanding the meaning of this word is extremely important to understanding God's purpose in allowing conflict. It was a word used to distinguish genuine currency from counterfeit currency. There was no national mint at this time in history. Nations made money from precious metals, melted down, and poured into molds to make coins. Once the coins cooled, it was necessary to smooth off the uneven edges. Since the coins were soft, someone could shave them down to take these rough edges off. Some coin makers would shave off more than they should in order to save the precious metal and increase their profits. The coins that did not measure up in weight were considered counterfeit (*adokimos*). The coins that were the correct weight were called *dokimos* or "approved."

Therefore, conflict must exist in the church and relationships so those involved can be observed and it can be determined if they are genuinely what they profess to be. If they are willing to resolve conflict, love one another, forgive one another, and do that which is right before God, then they are genuine Christians.

Secondly, Christ allows conflict in relationships so Christians can teach righteousness by modeling it. This means that the genuine Christian teaches the right things to do by doing the right things before others. This is one of the reasons God commands Christians to study the Word of God so they will know what God wants them to do in certain situations of life and so they can be "approved unto God" (the same Greek word *dokimos* is used here). In other words, we are to study God's Word so that we need not be ashamed before God and His people because we failed to act the way God expects.

"[5] But with many of them God was not well pleased: for they were overthrown in the wilderness. [6] Now these things were our examples, to the intent we should not lust after evil things, as they also lusted. [7] Neither be ye idolaters, as *were* some of them; as it is written, The people sat down to eat and drink, and rose up to play. [8] Neither let us commit fornication, as some of them committed, and fell in one day three and twenty thousand. [9] Neither let us tempt Christ, as some of them also tempted, and were destroyed of serpents. [10] Neither murmur ye, as some of them also murmured, and were destroyed of the destroyer. [11] Now all these things happened unto them for ensamples: and they are written for our admonition, upon whom the ends of the world are come. [12] Wherefore let him that thinketh he standeth take heed lest he fall. [13] There hath no temptation taken you but such as is common to man: but God *is* faithful, who will not suffer you to be tempted above that ye are able; but will with the temptation also make a way to escape, that ye may be able to bear *it*. [14] Wherefore, my dearly beloved, flee from idolatry" (I Corinthians 10:5-14).

The word "examples" in verse six is from the Greek word *tupos* (too'-pos). As used in this context, it refers to the failures of God's people in their actions and their lives that served as admonitions and warnings against repeating the same failures. As Christians, we will be models of righteousness or models of unrighteousness. In either case, we lead people directly and indirectly.

If you intend to disarm Satan's ability to use conflict to lure you out from under God's wings (from within His revealed will) of protection and security, you will need to decide to view conflict as an opportunity. You will then need to determine to always do what is right within that conflict. There are three important things to remember about conflict management:

1. Observe counterfeit Christians in conflict with one another. Observe how they *react* in the conflict. Determine to direct them to do what is right in the future.
2. Teach conflict management by modeling righteousness (doing what is right) by your actions.
3. Study God's Word to learn what God wants you to do in every situation of life (especially conflict) and then do what is right to show yourself "approved" (genuine) before Him.

If you have determined that you have repeatedly shown yourself to be a *counterfeit* Christian by your response to people in conflict, correct that by humbling yourself, seeking their forgiveness, and acknowledging your failure before them and God. If you are unwilling to do that, it only gives further evidence of your being a *counterfeit* Christian.

Handfuls On Purpose
Studies in the Book of Ruth
Chapter Thirteen
Dealing with Conflict and Problems God's Way

1. How can you use the everyday conflict in your life, such as your children's disobedience, to teach them the things God wants them to learn about life and life's trials and problems?

2. Read Romans 2:4. The Word of God tells us it is God's goodness that leads us to repentance. Why is it so important to God that every act of sin and disobedience end with confession and repentance?

3. If every act of sin does not end with confession and repentance, has that conflict been resolved?

4. When a believer refuses to seek to resolve the conflict of sin through confession and repentance is he also refusing God's sheltering protection?

5. Compare the modern Christian with the idea of a person who attended school with perfect attendance, was never late, but who refused to do the assignments (do the work) or take the tests.

6. Can we ever discover what we have learned if we are never tested?

7. How did Elimelech and Naomi respond to God's testing and discipline in Ruth chapter one?

8. According to Romans 2:4, what could have Elimelech and Naomi expected from God's discipline in their lives?

9. When the Christian refuses to confess sin and repent, he remains outside of God's will. According to I Peter 5:8-9, who will be eating away at you while you remain outside of God's will and what does that mean?

10. Read I Corinthians 11:19. Discuss the meaning of the word "heresies."

11. Discuss why God must allow "heresies" to regularly arise in a local church.

12. Discuss the meaning of the word "approved" in I Corinthians 11:19.

13. Discuss how understanding the word "approved" helps us understand God's purposes in allowing conflict and problems to exist in our personal lives and in a local church.

14. Discuss the concept of modeling righteousness in the context of why God allows conflict to exist in our lives.

15. Read II Timothy 2:15. How does the study of the Word of God relate to the believer's modeling of righteousness?

16. Read I Corinthians 10:5-14. Discuss the meaning of the word "examples" from verse six. Discuss how this meaning relates to the believer as both a model of righteousness and of unrighteousness.

Handfuls On Purpose
Studies in the Book of Ruth
Chapter Fourteen
Gleaning in the Field of God's Love

"¹³ Then she said, Let me find favour in thy sight, my lord; for that thou hast comforted me, and for that thou hast spoken friendly {*to the heart*} unto thine handmaid, though I be not like unto one of thine handmaidens. ¹⁴ And Boaz said unto her, At mealtime come thou hither, and eat of the bread, and dip thy morsel in the vinegar. And she sat beside the reapers: and he reached her parched *corn*, and she did eat, and was sufficed, and left. ¹⁵ And when she was risen up to glean, Boaz commanded his young men, saying, Let her glean even among the sheaves, and reproach {*shame*} her not: ¹⁶ And let fall also *some* of the handfuls of purpose for her, and leave *them*, that she may glean *them*, and rebuke her not" (Ruth 2:13-16).

Love is one of God's many attributes (qualities or characteristics). We know love as a *communicable attribute*. This means love is one of God's attributes that He wants to transfer to the lives of His children. It is one of the most difficult practices to learn, because it is the opposite of what we are. Humanity by nature (fallen) is almost completely preoccupied with himself (*self-love*). Biblical love (*God-kind* love) preoccupies itself with meeting the needs of others.

Another problem with understanding love is that man has redefined its meaning to be an *emotion*. To most people, love is something they *feel*. For others, love is something they *fall into* or *out of*. For a large group of people, love is synonymous with sex.

It is obvious why God speaks so often about love in His Word - giving many examples of it rather than trying to define it. The reason for this is that apart from the examples of love in the Bible, it is really totally beyond us. Love is a supernatural expression of who God is. Restoring its reality in the lives of believers is a major aspect of restoring the image of God in our lives.

Boaz loved Ruth, but his love had little to do with his *emotions* or *feelings*. It was not *love at first sight* or something *into* which he *fell*. Boaz loved Ruth because Boaz was a loving, caring, and gentle man. We do not define love by what we *feel*. We define love by what we *are*. We define love by the actions of our life because of what we are. Love always does the right things (the best things) for those we love. To do anything else is to manifest an ignorance and inability to love. To love biblically is to reveal both the knowledge of God and His supernatural working in our lives.

> "[8] He that loveth not knoweth not God; for God is love. [9] In this was manifested the love of God toward us, because that God sent his only begotten Son into the world, that we might live through him. [10] Herein is love, not that we loved God, but that he loved us, and sent his Son *to be* the propitiation for our sins. [11] Beloved, if God so loved us, we ought also to love one another. [12] No man hath seen God at any time. If we love one another, God dwelleth in us, and his love is perfected in us. [13] Hereby know we that we dwell in him, and he in us, because he hath given us of his Spirit" (I John 4:8-13).

God's love (the kind of love that *God is*) is not defined by what He feels, but by what He is. He does what He does (actions of love) because of what He is. Feelings and actions flow from the well of what we are on the inside. Only God can produce love (the kind of love God is). He is its only source

> "[22] But the fruit of the Spirit is love, joy, peace, longsuffering, gentleness, goodness, faith, [23] Meekness, temperance: against such there is no law. [24] And they that are Christ's have crucified the flesh with the affections and lusts" (Galatians 5:22-24).

How do we make visible what we *are*? How do we make love visible (Ruth 2:13)?

We make love visible by what we do for others. Boaz shows great love for Ruth in this text. His *actions* reveal his love. Love always describes an *action* that benefits another person. Love never describes an *emotion* or *feeling*. There may be feelings and emotions that accompany love, which are often confused as love, but those emotions or feelings are not love.

When Ruth says, "Let me find favour in thy sight" (2:13), she is making a statement of hope. It might be paraphrased, "May I continue to find favour, based upon your past performance or actions." Ruth is not making a request of Boaz. It was a way in which a Hebrew woman implied gratitude for what someone did for her. Ruth was expressing sincere gratitude for what Boaz had already done for her. We have a similar reply from Hannah to Eli after he had blessed her in I Samuel 1:18.

> "And she said, Let thine handmaid find grace in thy sight. So the woman went her way, and did eat, and her countenance was no more *sad*" (I Samuel 1:18).

In Ruth's next statement, she acknowledges that Boaz loves her. The words, "Thou has comforted me" (not just *made me feel good*) designate something done that meets a specific need of someone oppressed or distressed. In other words, Boaz sacrificed some aspect of himself to meet the needs of another.

Real love meets needs. This is the definition of ministry.

We cannot define biblical ministry apart from biblical love. To determine if we love someone, we might ask ourselves the question, "What am I doing to help the person I say I love to become a better person?" Or, "What need have I met in this person's life that has helped him become a better person or realize his potential in Jesus Christ? Two things measure the reality of a person's love for another person:

1. What you are <u>doing</u> to help another person
2. What you <u>sacrifice</u> to accomplish it

If you do not love, you will not minister to others. If you do not minister to others, you do not love. You may force yourself to do ministry out of obligation or because of perceived pressure from Christian peers, but this kind of ministry becomes self-serving and is not done out of biblical love. When we know the kind of sacrificial, others-serving kind of love that God is, we seek to replicate that kind of love in our own lives.

"He that loveth not knoweth not God; for God is love" (I John 4:8).

When it comes to ministry, most people want to be involved in the *big things*, but few are willing to do the *little things* that go unnoticed. It is not an act of love if what we do is to earn personal praise or glory. It is an act of selfishness. Someone has said, "It is amazing what we can accomplish if we do not care who gets credit for it."

> "[31] When the Son of man shall come in his glory, and all the holy angels with him, then shall he sit upon the throne of his glory: [32] And before him shall be gathered all nations: and he shall separate them one from another, as a shepherd divideth *his* sheep from the goats: [33] And he shall set the sheep on his right hand, but the goats on the left. [34] Then shall the King say unto them on his right hand, Come, ye blessed of my Father, inherit the kingdom prepared for you from the foundation of the world: [35] For I was an hungred, and ye gave me meat: I was thirsty, and ye gave me drink: I was a stranger, and ye took me in: [36] Naked, and ye clothed me: I was sick, and ye visited me: I was in prison, and ye came unto me. [37] Then shall the righteous answer him, saying, Lord, when saw we thee an hungred, and fed *thee*? or thirsty, and gave *thee* drink? [38] When saw we thee a stranger, and took *thee* in? or naked, and clothed *thee*? [39] Or when saw we thee sick, or in prison, and came unto thee? [40] And the King shall answer and say unto them, Verily I say unto you, Inasmuch as ye have done *it* unto one of the least of these my brethren, ye have done *it* unto me. [41] Then shall he say also unto them on the left hand, Depart from me, ye cursed, into everlasting fire, prepared for the devil and his angels: [42] For I was an hungred, and ye gave me no meat: I was thirsty, and ye gave me no drink: [43] I was a stranger, and ye took me not in: naked, and ye clothed me not: sick, and in prison, and ye visited me not. [44] Then shall they also answer him, saying, Lord, when saw we thee an hungred, or athirst, or a stranger, or naked, or sick, or in prison, and did not minister unto thee? [45] Then shall he answer them, saying, Verily I say unto you, Inasmuch as ye did *it* not to one of the least of these, ye did *it* not to me. [46] And these shall go away into everlasting punishment: but the righteous into life eternal" (Matthew 25:31-46).

This text does not refer to the *Social Gospel*. The text refers Christ dividing true believers ("سheep") from false believers ("goats") by what people do towards the nation of Israel during the seven year Tribulation and before the second coming of Christ at Armageddon (v. 31). How does Christ divide the real disciples ("sheep") from false disciples ("goats")? He divides them by their actions of love towards persecuted Israel. Just like in the case of Boaz, he met *real needs*.

Is this text teaching socialism? Is the faithful Christian responsible to feed the starving masses in the world? Is the faithful Christian responsible to provide housing and clothing for the homeless? No, that interpretation takes this portion of Scripture completely out of its dispensational context and applies it to present sociological issues. The text does not mean the believer is responsible for every drug addict, drunkard, or shiftless bum who refuses to work. The Bible says if a man (Christian) refuses to work, he should not eat of the common (communion) meal (II Thessalonians 3:10).

Secondly, a believer is not responsible for those who reject the Gospel and who reject Jesus Christ and the authority of His Word over their lives. They are receiving the natural consequences of a chosen life of sin (Romans 1:24-32 and II Thessalonians 3:6-13). On the other hand, when someone is really trying to live for the Lord and has some real needs, the believer should try to do what he can to help that person.

The first and greatest need of any person is the need to be saved. God meets that need through His love. God provides salvation as a gift of His grace through faith in the finished sacrifice of Christ. He does this by satisfying our death sentence on the Cross of Calvary. Christians need to give that love to the whole "world."

The second greatest need of all people is the need to be loved. That need is met in hundreds of ways by hundreds of different people as they work together to help one another restore the image of God in each other's lives.

"For thou has spoken friendly" (Ruth 2:13) reveals another important aspect of biblical love.

This statement could be literally phrased, "For thou has spoken to the heart." Boaz's love went far beyond meeting the physical and material needs of Ruth. He sought to meet her spiritual needs (the needs of her heart) as well. Biblical love sees beyond the physical and material needs, although it does not ignore those needs.

> "[14] What *doth it* profit, my brethren, though a man say he hath faith, and have not works? can faith save him? [15] If a brother or sister be naked, and destitute of daily food, [16] And one of you say unto them, Depart in peace, be *ye* warmed and filled; notwithstanding ye give

them not those things which are needful to the body; what *doth it profit?* [17] Even so faith, if it hath not works, is dead, being alone. [18] Yea, a man may say, Thou hast faith, and I have works: shew me thy faith without thy works, and I will shew thee my faith by my works" (James 2:14-18).

The central problem with the common misinterpretation of this text is the false teaching of the universal *fatherhood* of God and the universal *brotherhood* of man. God created one man named Adam. All other human beings are the product of procreation, not creation. God fathered one Son named Jesus. To become a child of God a person must be "born again" by grace through faith in the "finished" propitiatory work of Christ and His resurrection out from the dead. That *new birth* is what makes us brothers and sisters "in Christ." James 2:15 refers to those individuals.

If you feed a hungry person, he will be hungry again tomorrow. Real love forces the believer to go beyond the obvious and external to deal with the inner man and the spiritual failures that bring the lost person to his human predicament. The only correction for ignorance is education. The only correction for moral turpitude is confession, repentance, and that person's acknowledgment of his need of salvation to be "born again."

"Come thou hither" (Ruth 2:14).

These words from Boaz instruct Ruth to draw near to him. Herein lays the big difference between the "love of this world" and the love of God. The love of this world is preoccupied with things. The love of Christ is preoccupied with people. Real love (ministry) is pouring out what God has given you of Himself into another person's life.

> "[25] But Jesus called them *unto him*, and said, Ye know that the princes of the Gentiles exercise dominion over them, and they that are great exercise authority upon them. [26] But it shall not be so among you: but whosoever will be great among you, let him be your minister; [27] And whosoever will be chief among you, let him be your servant: [28] Even as the Son of man came not to be ministered unto, but to minister, and to give his life a ransom for many" (Matthew 20:25-28).

"Among the sheaves" (Ruth 2:15) and "even pull out some handfuls on purpose for her" (Ruth 2:16) – in these statements God reveals two things about love:

1. Real love is not concerned about recognition or applause. It is willing to be *secret*.
2. Real love is concerned about human dignity and self worth (this differs greatly from the humanistic idea of self-esteem).

If we love with the expectation of gratitude or with the idea that the person loved is indebted to us, that is not a gift of love, but a down-payment on a person's soul (*to make them indebted to us*). Biblical love does not indebt people to you. Real love frees people from indebtedness. Real love is always of grace or it is not love. Anything less takes the divine attribute out of God's love and prostitutes it, making it something contemptible.

When the believer serves God, it should be because he loves Him. God magnified His love at Calvary where He gave His only begotten Son to meet every single need of man for salvation. God magnified His love in the giving of the Holy Spirit to indwell the believer and to enable him to become what God expects him to be.

The love of God is magnified in the giving of His Word to humanity to provide all we need to teach us how to live righteously. In summary, God magnifies His love by *giving*. He did not need us. We need Him, so He gave of Himself to meet our desperate needs. We glorify God (*make His love known*) by the exhibition of the kind of love God is - by loving others the way He loved us.

Handfuls On Purpose
Studies in the Book of Ruth
Chapter Fourteen
Gleaning in the Field of God's Love

1. Discuss why biblical love is such a difficult thing to learn to do.

2. Discuss why *falling in love*, *falling out of love* or defining love as an *emotion* or *feeling* is totally out of harmony with biblical love.

3. Discuss why Boaz loved Ruth and why God loves you. Discuss how understanding this helps the believer define biblical love and practice it.

4. Read I John 4:8-13. Discuss the meaning of verse eight, especially dealing with the idea that feelings and actions flow from the well of what we are on the inside.

5. Read Galatians 5:22-24. Discuss the only true source of biblical love. Discuss how believers release love through their lives.

6. Read Ruth 2:13. Discuss how we make love visible.

7. Compare the statement of Ruth (2:13), "Let me find favour in thy sight," with the statement of Hannah to Eli in I Samuel 1:18 and Ziba to King David in II Samuel 16:4. Discuss what these statements are intended to reflect about those making them.

8. What does Ruth's statement, "Thou hast comforted me" (Ruth 2:13), reveal to us about biblical love? What is the meaning of these words?

9. Give the two things by which God measures the reality of a person's love for another person.

10. Discuss why most people want to be involved in the *big things* of ministry.

11. Read Matthew 25:31-46. Discuss how Christ divides His real disciples ("sheep") from false disciples ("goats").

12. Discuss the first and greatest need of any person. Discuss how Christians can meet that need.

13. Discuss the second greatest need of all people. Discuss how Christians can meet that need.

14. Discuss the words, "For thou hast spoken friendly" in Ruth 2:13, and what this reveals about Boaz's love for Ruth. How should that truth be applied through the lives of all believers?

15. Discuss the spiritual significance of the words, "Come thou hither" in Ruth 2:14, as this defines biblical love.

16. Discuss the spiritual significance of the words, "Among the sheaves" in Ruth 2:15 and "Even pull out some handfuls on purpose for her" in Ruth 2:16. Discuss what two things these two statements reveal about biblical love.

17. Discuss the error in doing good deeds with the expectation of someone repaying us or having someone indebted to you for what you have done.

Handfuls On Purpose
Studies in the Book of Ruth
Chapter Fifteen
Understanding the Seasons of the Soul

"[17] So she gleaned in the field until even, and beat out that she had gleaned: and it was about an ephah of barley. [18] And she took *it* up, and went into the city: and her mother in law saw what she had gleaned: and she brought forth, and gave to her that she had reserved after she was sufficed. [19] And her mother in law said unto her, Where hast thou gleaned to day? and where wroughtest thou? blessed be he that did take knowledge of thee. And she shewed her mother in law with whom she had wrought, and said, The man's name with whom I wrought to day *is* Boaz. [20] And Naomi said unto her daughter in law, Blessed *be* he of the LORD, who hath not left off his kindness to the living and to the dead. And Naomi said unto her, The man *is* near of kin unto us, one of our next kinsmen. [21] And Ruth the Moabitess said, He said unto me also, Thou shalt keep fast by my young men, until they have ended all my harvest. [22] And Naomi said unto Ruth her daughter in law, *It is* good, my daughter, that thou go out with his maidens, that they meet thee not in any other field. [23] So she kept fast by the maidens of Boaz to glean unto the end of barley harvest and of wheat harvest; and dwelt with her mother in law" (Ruth 2:17-23).

Ruth 2:23 gives us a great deal of information, but in order to utilize that information we must understand some technical things about the biblical culture of Israel and their religious calendar. The Jewish seasonal calendar was called the *Gezer Calendar*. According to that calendar, the harvest season started in the fourth month (Nibib) with the Passover.

Part of the Passover celebration (a weeklong period) was the offering of the "first fruits" of the barley harvest. The harvest season lasted exactly seven weeks (49 days). It began on a Sabbath and ended on a Sabbath, what we call Saturday. God called the fiftieth day (the first day after the harvest season) the Day of Pentecost. The Day of Pentecost was always a Sunday.

The death, burial, resurrection, and ascension of Christ Jesus and the coming of the Holy Spirit all fell within this period of time called the *Harvest Season*. Jesus was the "first fruits" of the resurrection. All those saved from the Day of Pentecost (Acts 2:1) to the rapture (I Thessalonians 4:16-17) are the first *harvest of souls* to glorification (called "fruit" in the Bible). The gleaning and completion of the third phase of the "first resurrection" will be the saved martyrs of the Tribulation (Revelation 20:4-6).

> "[20] But now is Christ risen from the dead, *and* become the firstfruits of them that slept. [21] For since by man *came* death, by man *came* also the resurrection of the dead. [22] For as in Adam all die, even so in Christ shall all be made alive. [23] But every man in his own order: Christ the firstfruits; afterward they that are Christ's at his coming" (I Corinthians 15:20-23).

What we want to see in this text is the fact that God has Eschatological *seasons of the soul*. This is God's dispensational cycle of the *harvest of souls*. We might call these dispensations *windows of spiritual opportunity*. The whole Church Age is a *window of opportunity*. The harvest season of Ruth 2:23 is typical of the whole Church Age and Ruth is typical of all believers who trust in Christ from the day of Pentecost to the completion of the Tribulation.

There are also individual seasons *of the soul* in the life of every believer. This is the working of God in the lives of individuals to bring them to spiritual maturity and full productivity. God intends to produce a continuum from one generation of believers to succeeding generations. Believers are to work with God on their own spiritual growth and then in the harvesting of souls of others belonging to their lifespan.

God never ceases in His work of bringing individual Christians to salvation, to spiritual maturity, and to full productivity in their lives.

> "[9] And immediately the man was made whole, and took up his bed, and walked: and on the same day was the sabbath. [10] The Jews therefore said unto him that was cured, It is the sabbath day: it is not lawful for thee to carry *thy* bed. [11] He answered them, He that made me whole, the same said unto me, Take up thy bed, and walk. [12] Then asked they him, What man is that which said unto thee, Take up thy bed, and walk? [13] And he that was healed wist not who it was: for Jesus had conveyed himself away, a multitude being in *that* place. [14] Afterward Jesus findeth him in the temple, and said unto him, Behold, thou art made whole: sin no more, lest a worse thing

come unto thee. [15] The man departed, and told the Jews that it was Jesus, which had made him whole. [16] And therefore did the Jews persecute Jesus, and sought to slay him, because he had done these things on the sabbath day. [17] But Jesus answered them, My Father worketh hitherto, and I work. [18] Therefore the Jews sought the more to kill him, because he not only had broken the sabbath, but said also that God was his Father, making himself equal with God" (John 5:9-18).

Jesus healed on the Sabbath. Therefore, the apostate religious leaders of Israel sought to have Jesus killed because they claimed He broke the Sabbath (an offense worthy of death). To answer their accusation against Him, Jesus makes a remarkable statement that made Him equal with God (v. 17). Paraphrasing what Jesus said, "From the end of creation until now, the Father has never ceased His working and neither have I." Jesus is the Creator. Everything in this world exists and consists by Jesus Christ.

"[15] Who is the image of the invisible God, the firstborn of every creature: [16] For by him were all things created, that are in heaven, and that are in earth, visible and invisible, whether *they be* thrones, or dominions, or principalities, or powers: all things were created by him, and for him: [17] And he is before all things, and by him all things consist" (Colossians 1:15-17).

The word "consist" is from the Greek word *sunistao* (soon-is-tah'-o) meaning *to put things together or unite parts into a whole.* The idea is that Jesus is not only the Creator, but also that without Him everything would fall apart. Just stop for a moment and ask yourself where your life would be apart from God's continual intervention and working to keep you from sin and self-destruction. Jesus is always (constantly) working in each of our lives to lift us out of the *slime pits of sin* and advance us to higher spiritual ground.

All that happened in Ruth and Naomi's lives up to this point were *seasons of their souls,* preparing them for a higher purpose in life. In order for Ruth (and us) to realize God's higher purpose (His "handfuls on purpose"), Ruth had to cooperate with God's working in her life. She had to *grow spiritually.* In order for God to accomplish His purposes in our lives and in order for us to realize our fullest productivity for the cause of Christ, we each must work with God to search out and remove all barriers of sin.

"^{1} I am the true vine, and my Father is the husbandman. ^{2} Every branch in me that beareth not fruit he taketh away: and every *branch* that beareth fruit, he purgeth it, that it may bring forth more fruit. ^{3} Now ye are clean through the word which I have spoken unto you. ^{4} Abide in me, and I in you. As the branch cannot bear fruit of itself, except it abide in the vine; no more can ye, except ye abide in me. ^{5} I am the vine, ye *are* the branches: He that abideth in me, and I in him, the same bringeth forth much fruit: for without me {*severed from me*} ye can do nothing. ^{6} If a man abide not in me, he is cast forth as a branch, and is withered; and men gather them, and cast *them* into the fire, and they are burned. ^{7} If ye abide in me, and my words abide in you, ye shall ask what ye will, and it shall be done unto you. ^{8} Herein is my Father glorified, that ye bear much fruit; so shall ye be my disciples" (John 15:1-8).

There must be "purging" of anything in our life that keeps us from being what God wants us to be. There can be no sin, attitude, nor idol of the heart that is allowed to remain as a barrier to our full development as Christians. Becoming the kind of person God can use will not happen by accident. The harvest of God's blessings ("fruit") will only take place when the *seasons of our soul* have come to the place of full spiritual maturity in Christ.

In the early development of Ruth's life (when she was still gleaning, 2:17) she brought home an "ephah" of barley grain (about a five-gallon pail full). God had showered her with blessings, but she had to learn to pick them up. She had to work hard to glean that much, but we can only see our spiritual bounty in Christ when we see it from the perspective of our spiritual bankruptcy without Him.

As the wife of Boaz, Ruth would be co-owner of the whole harvest. It is in our relationship with Christ that we finally realize our full potential as Christians. God is constantly working to bring us into that spiritual relationship with Christ (the biblical word for that relationship is "fellowship") where we learn to love Him more than life itself. That is when we will begin to realize our full potential in Christ and bring forth a harvest.

In order for God to bless a believer's life to the fullest potential, that believer must be where God wants him to be (in "fellowship," I John 1:3-7) AND he must be doing what God wants him to be doing ("the work of the ministry," Ephesians 4:12).

Many Christians just cannot *get it together* spiritually. They think being in "fellowship" with God is when they are not living in sin, have their sin confessed, and have their lives right. That is only half of what "fellowship" with God is. "Fellowship" refers to a *partnership* with God. The other half is involving one's self in the "work of the ministry." The Christian has to be where God wants him to be spiritually, doing what God wants him to do.

I often wonder how much of God's ripe harvest in the *seasons of the soul* lie rotting in the harvest field because those He intended to harvest the fruit are still lying in bed, out playing, watching a T.V. show, or busy with some hobby. We pray for God's blessings and, because of our idleness, those blessings lie wasting away.

We each are an important part of a broad scope of God's plan of the harvest of souls.

> "[12] Wherefore, my beloved, as ye have always obeyed, not as in my presence only, but now much more in my absence, work out your own salvation with fear and trembling. [13] For it is God which worketh in you both to will and to do of *his* good pleasure. [14] Do all things without murmurings and disputings: [15] That ye may be blameless and harmless, the sons of God, without rebuke, in the midst of a crooked and perverse nation, among whom ye shine as lights in the world; [16] Holding forth the word of life; that I may rejoice in the day of Christ, that I have not run in vain, neither laboured in vain" (Philippians 2:12-16).

Each believer is a part of a larger whole (the *body principle* of I Corinthians 12 and Romans 12). What we are and where we are in our spiritual growth as Christians will determine to a great deal our effectiveness to accomplish the overall plan of God in the locality in which we live. Take one little *drive wheel* out of the greatest timepiece in the world and it will not accomplish what it was intended to do. Take a piano with one key out of tune and it will throw off the harmony of a whole piece of music.

God is constantly working (2:13) in our lives to bring us into full harmony with His Word and His will. What Paul says in Ephesians 5:16 must become the priority of our lives if we are ever going to realize the full potential of the *seasons of the soul* and the harvest of God's fruit.

"¹ Be ye therefore followers of God, as dear children; ² And walk in love, as Christ also hath loved us, and hath given himself for us an offering and a sacrifice to God for a sweetsmelling savour. ³ But fornication, and all uncleanness, or covetousness, let it not be once named among you, as becometh saints; ⁴ Neither filthiness, nor foolish talking, nor jesting, which are not convenient: but rather giving of thanks. ⁵ For this ye know, that no whoremonger, nor unclean person, nor covetous man, who is an idolater, hath any inheritance in the kingdom of Christ and of God. ⁶ Let no man deceive you with vain words: for because of these things cometh the wrath of God upon the children of disobedience {*unbelief*}. ⁷ Be not ye therefore partakers with them. ⁸ For ye were sometimes darkness, but now *are ye* light in the Lord: walk as children of light: ⁹ (For the fruit of the Spirit *is* in all goodness and righteousness and truth;) ¹⁰ Proving what is acceptable unto the Lord. ¹¹ And have no fellowship with the unfruitful works of darkness, but rather reprove *them*. ¹² For it is a shame even to speak of those things which are done of them in secret. ¹³ But all things that are reproved are made manifest by the light: for whatsoever doth make manifest is light. ¹⁴ Wherefore he saith, Awake thou that sleepest, and arise from the dead, and Christ shall give thee light. ¹⁵ See then that ye walk circumspectly, not as fools, but as wise, ¹⁶ Redeeming the time, because the days are evil. ¹⁷ Wherefore be ye not unwise, but understanding what the will of the Lord *is*" (Ephesians 5:1-17).

Handfuls On Purpose
Studies in the Book of Ruth
Chapter Fifteen
Understanding the Seasons of the Soul

1. The Jewish seasonal calendar was called as the *Gezer Calendar*. What celebration was going on at the beginning of barley harvest?

2. How long did the harvest season last?

3. What was the day after harvest season called and on what day did it always fall?

4. What is the New Testament significance in the correlation of all of this?

5. What are some of the *seasons of the soul* in your own life where God has moved you from one place of growth to a *higher plane* or *higher walk* with Him? What was necessary (what were the circumstances) that God used to bring you to that place?

6. Read John 5:9-17. Has God ever ceased His working in your life to bring you to the place where He can use you for His intended purpose?

7. Could Ruth have harvested the blessings of God in this *season of her soul* if she had not been where God wanted her, doing what God wanted her to do?

8. How does this principle apply to you?

9. Read John 15:1-8. Do you think that you have some barriers to growth that you must remove to realize God's blessings in your *seasons of the soul*?

10. Read Ruth 2:17. Did that "ephah" of barley just fall into Ruth's lap or did she have to work hard to gather God's blessings for her?

11. How many of God's blessings for your life are rotting on the ground, never gathered, never used?

12. Read Philippians 2:12-16. Are you a *missing gear* in God's plan?

13. What decision do you need to make today and everyday so that this will never happen again?

Handfuls On Purpose
Studies in the Book of Ruth
Chapter Sixteen
Claiming Redemption by Claiming Our Redeemer

"¹ Then Naomi her mother in law said unto her, My daughter, shall I not seek rest for thee, that it may be well with thee? ² And now *is* not Boaz of our kindred, with whose maidens thou wast? Behold, he winnoweth barley to night in the threshingfloor. ³ Wash thyself therefore, and anoint thee, and put thy raiment upon thee, and get thee down to the floor: *but* make not thyself known unto the man, until he shall have done eating and drinking. ⁴ And it shall be, when he lieth down, that thou shalt mark the place where he shall lie, and thou shalt go in, and uncover {*lift up the clothes that are on*} his feet, and lay thee down; and he will tell thee what thou shalt do. ⁵ And she said unto her, All that thou sayest unto me I will do. ⁶ And she went down unto the floor, and did according to all that her mother in law bade her. ⁷ And when Boaz had eaten and drunk, and his heart was merry, he went to lie down at the end of the heap of corn: and she came softly, and uncovered his feet, and laid her down. ⁸ And it came to pass at midnight, that the man was afraid, and turned himself: and, behold, a woman lay at his feet. ⁹ And he said, Who *art* thou? And she answered, I *am* Ruth thine handmaid: spread therefore thy skirt over thine handmaid; for thou *art* a near kinsman {*one that has the right to redeem*}. ¹⁰ And he said, Blessed *be* thou of the LORD, my daughter: *for* thou hast shewed more kindness in the latter end than at the beginning, inasmuch as thou followedst not young men, whether poor or rich. ¹¹ And now, my daughter, fear not; I will do to thee all that thou requirest: for all the city of my people doth know that thou *art* a virtuous woman" (Ruth 3:1-11).

How to be saved is one of the most misunderstood doctrines in the Bible. For some people, salvation is something they *earn* through good deeds. For others salvation is something they think they *deserve* because of things they have done (or have not done). Many others think salvation is some type of mystical or spiritual enlightenment that just happens to them at the end of a quest for some special knowledge or event in their life. Christ understood the satanic confusion that would evolve regarding salvation. He gave the following warning:

"*²¹* Not every one that saith unto me, Lord, Lord, shall enter into the kingdom of heaven; but he that doeth the will of my Father which is in heaven. *²²* Many will say to me in that day, Lord, Lord, have we not prophesied in thy name? and in thy name have cast out devils? and in thy name done many wonderful works? *²³* And then will I profess unto them, I never knew you: depart from me, ye that work iniquity. *²⁴* Therefore whosoever heareth these sayings of mine, and doeth them, I will liken him unto a wise man, which built his house upon a rock: *²⁵* And the rain descended, and the floods came, and the winds blew, and beat upon that house; and it fell not: for it was founded upon a rock. *²⁶* And every one that heareth these sayings of mine, and doeth them not, shall be likened unto a foolish man, which built his house upon the sand: *²⁷* And the rain descended, and the floods came, and the winds blew, and beat upon that house; and it fell: and great was the fall of it" (Matthew 7:21-27).

The Bible clearly teaches that salvation is not something we can *earn*, something we *deserve*, or something that just *happens* by osmosis. Being saved is a gift of God that comes totally undeserved (by grace; Ephesians 2:8-9). Being saved is an act of God whereby He removes the repentant sinner from a position of eminent danger and insecurity to a position of absolute safety and perfect security. This fits well with the idea of redemption found in the book of Ruth. Yet, salvation is a gift that we MUST receive.

Salvation is the result of an intelligent decision based upon understanding our need and the provision made for our redemption by Jesus Christ (our Redeemer). Jesus makes this provision through His life, death, and resurrection. Salvation is a gift of God's grace that we receive by absolute faith in the substitutionary work of Christ on our behalf. We receive the gift of salvation by believing the Gospel and receiving the person of Jesus Christ as our Lord. He is our salvation. Jesus, the person, the eternal Son of God is our salvation. Salvation is always and only in the person of Jesus Christ.

"*¹¹* For the grace of God that bringeth salvation hath appeared to all men, *¹²* Teaching us that, denying ungodliness and worldly lusts, we should live soberly, righteously, and godly, in this present world; *¹³* Looking for that blessed hope, and the glorious appearing {*the appearance of the glory*} of the great God and our Saviour Jesus Christ;" (Titus 2:11-13).

"Neither is there salvation in any other: for there is none other name under heaven given among men, whereby we must be saved" (Acts 4:12).

Receiving Christ is receiving both the Redeemer and His redemption. A person cannot receive redemption without receiving the Redeemer and who He is. He is Lord! This is not about *giving your life to Christ*. Your life is already His. He already has absolute authority over both your life and your soul. Receiving Christ and confessing Him as your Lord is acknowledging your understanding of the reality that your life and soul belong to Jesus.

"[11] He came unto his own, and his own received him not. [12] But as many as received him, to them gave he power to become the sons of God, *even* to them that believe on his name: [13] Which were born, not of blood, nor of the will of the flesh, nor of the will of man, but of God" (John 1:11-13).

With these truths in mind, we can pick up the story in Ruth 3:1. Ruth has just returned home from gleaning in the fields of Boaz. It was hot and dirty work. She had already beaten the grain from the stocks. She had probably just finished working a sixteen hour day. She is tired, sweaty, and dirty.

Now we find Naomi and Ruth making plans to claim Boaz as their kinsman redeemer. In his redemption, they will find "rest" (a safe shelter meaning protection and security). According to Ruth 3:2, Boaz was *winnowing barley* at the *threshing floor*. The *threshing floor* was a hard parched clay circular on top of a hill that was hard as concrete. In the late afternoon, a breeze would begin to blow and the threshing and winnowing would begin. As long as the wind continued to blow, the threshing and winnowing would continue. This would often extend late into the night and early morning. After this long day, Boaz was still at the threshing floor working.

It would appear from Ruth 3:2-4 that Boaz was alone at the *threshing floor*. Of course, that was not the case. This was a time of feasting. All the household of Boaz would camp around the *threshing floor*. There would have been many people present, perhaps hundreds. This is important in order to understand that there was nothing inappropriate here between Ruth and Boaz.

After the feast and work was over for the day, the men would sleep around the grain pile using it as a backrest with their feet sticking out from it like spokes on a giant wagon wheel. They encircled the entire grain pile this way to keep thieves from sneaking up in the dark and stealing the grain.

As we read our story, Naomi instructed Ruth to wait until Boaz has finished eating and while the lamp was remained lit. Then, she was to note where he laid down at the grain pile. Then, after Boaz was asleep, Ruth was to go and quietly lay down at Boaz's feet. In doing so, Ruth did two things:

1. She was officially making her request of him to be her redeemer.
2. To lay down at his feet signified complete submission to Him (Lordship).

According to Ruth 3:8, Boaz was startled out of his sleep about midnight by something and discovers Ruth at his feet. Ruth requests Boaz to spread his "skirt over thine handmaiden (Ruth 3:9). The Hebrew is really *spread thy wing (*kanaph - *kaw-nawf"*). It is a Hebrew idiom referring to sheltering protection (compare Ruth 2:2; Psalm 17:8, 36:7, 91:4). The real meaning is that Ruth was proposing marriage. She was laying claim to her redeemer and the redemption that was her gift from God in him.

In Ruth 3:10, Boaz commends Ruth for choosing him rather then one of the younger men and he promises her he will do everything he can to redeem her. What a blessing when we consider the extremes to which Jesus has gone to redeem us.

> "Who gave himself for us, that he might redeem us from all iniquity, and purify unto himself a peculiar people, zealous of good works" (Titus 2:14).

The redemption of humanity was the plan of God from the very beginning before God ever created man. We know this from Galatians 4:4-5.

> "[4] But when the fulness of the time was come, God sent forth his Son, made of a woman, made under the law, [5] To redeem them that were under the law, that we might receive the adoption of sons" (Galatians 4:4-5).

We could paraphrase the words "fullness of time" (pleroma chromos - *play'-ro-mah khron'-os*) - *when time was fully prepared to deliver*. The point of reference takes us back to Genesis 3:15 when God promised a Redeemer for His fallen Creation. God made Creation *pregnant* with His promise. When the necessary time was fulfilled, Messiah was born "made of a woman" (v. 4). Humanity needed a *kinsman redeemer*, so the eternal Son of God became the Son of man.

That means perfect God and perfect Man were united in one body. That fact is important because "made under the Law" means Jesus Christ (in His humanity) shared the communion of all mankind under the Law. That carries with it all the obligations and responsibilities of the Law. The good news is that Jesus Christ succeeded where every man has failed.

> "As it is written, There is none righteous, no, not one:" (Romans 3:10).

> "For all have sinned, and come short of the glory of God;" (Romans 3:23).

> "Who did no sin, neither was guile found in his mouth:" (I Peter 2:22).

> "For Christ also hath once suffered for sins, the just for the unjust, that he might bring us to God, being put to death in the flesh, but quickened by the Spirit:" (I Peter 3:18).

The central purpose of the incarnation (Galatians 4:5) was "to redeem them that were under the {*condemnation of the*} law" because all humanity failed and were guilty of breaking that Law. All were condemned to death because all are guilty of the capital crime of sin against God.

> "Now we know that what things soever the law saith, it saith to them who are under the law: that every mouth may be stopped, and all the world may become guilty before God" {*subject to the judgment of God, which judgment is a death sentence, Romans 6:23*} (Romans 3:19).

> "[9] That if thou shalt confess with thy mouth the Lord Jesus, and shalt believe in thine heart that God hath raised him from the dead, thou shalt be saved. [10] For with the heart man believeth unto righteousness; and with the mouth confession is made unto salvation" (Romans 10:9-10).

Why is the sinlessness of Christ so important? Salvation is in a person - the Son of God who became man. Why is it necessary to believe in the deity of Jesus Christ before anyone can be saved? If Jesus is not God then He was just another man. If He was just another man, He was born a sinner just like every descendant of Adam.

> "Wherefore, as by one man sin entered into the world, and death by sin; and so death passed upon all men, for that all have sinned:" (Romans 5:12).

One of the laws of redemption was that the person redeeming must not need redemption himself. The ability of Jesus to redeem (and the basis of salvation) is that He is sinless.

> "For he hath made him *to be* sin for us, who knew no sin; that we might be made the righteousness of God in him" (II Corinthians 5:21).

> "¹⁸ Forasmuch as ye know that ye were not redeemed with corruptible things, *as* silver and gold, from your vain conversation *received* by tradition from your fathers; ¹⁹ But with the precious blood of Christ, as of a lamb without blemish and without spot:" (I Peter 1:18-19).

A man can do nothing to redeem himself. He is absolutely depraved and completely bankrupt spiritually. All he can do is to humbly come to the feet of Jesus and accept the redemption He so freely offers. Have you claimed your redeemer? Come! Kneel at His feet in humble repentance. Call unto to Him believing the Gospel. "For whosoever shall call on the name of the Lord shall be saved" (Romans 10:13). His name is Jesus.

Handfuls On Purpose
Studies in the Book of Ruth
Chapter Sixteen
Claiming Redemption by Claiming Our Redeemer

1. Salvation (being saved) is a _____ of God that comes to us totally undeserved.

2. What does the word *grace* mean in the Bible (see Rom. 5:2)?

3. Salvation (being saved) is an act of God, whereby He moves the repentant sinner from a position of _____ danger and insecurity, to a _____ of absolute safety and perfect security.

4. Read Titus 2:10-14 and Acts 4:12. Why is it important to understand that salvation is in a person?

5. From Ruth 3:1, what does the word "rest" signify that Naomi is seeking for Ruth?

6. Read Ruth 3:2-4. Was Boaz alone at the *threshing floor*?

7. How did the men sleep at the *threshing floor*, what was their backrest and pillow, and why did they do so?

8. What were the two things signified by Ruth lying down at the feet of Boaz?

9. From Ruth 3:9, what is the real meaning of the Hebrew words translated, "spread therefore thy skirt over thine handmaid"?

10. Discuss the significance to the doctrine of salvation about why it is necessary for Jesus to be both deity and sinless.

11. Compare Romans 10:13 to Joel 2:32. In Joel the word "LORD" is the Hebrew Jehovah. Who then are you calling on to save you when you call on the name of Jesus?
   A. Are they the same?
   B. Have you called on Him (Jesus the God\man), in absolute faith, to save you?

Handfuls On Purpose
Studies in the Book of Ruth
Chapter Seventeen
The Miracle of Redemption

"[11] And now, my daughter, fear not; I will do to thee all that thou requirest: for all the city of my people doth know that thou *art* a virtuous woman. [12] And now it is true that I *am thy* near kinsman: howbeit there is a kinsman nearer than I. [13] Tarry this night, and it shall be in the morning, *that* if he will perform unto thee the part of a kinsman, well; let him do the kinsman's part: but if he will not do the part of a kinsman to thee, then will I do the part of a kinsman to thee, *as* the LORD liveth: lie down until the morning. [14] And she lay at his feet until the morning: and she rose up before one could know another. And he said, Let it not be known that a woman came into the floor. [15] Also he said, Bring the vail {*sheet or apron*} that *thou hast* upon thee, and hold it. And when she held it, he measured six *measures* of barley, and laid *it* on her: and she went into the city. [16] And when she came to her mother in law, she said, Who *art* thou, my daughter? And she told her all that the man had done to her. [17] And she said, These six *measures* of barley gave he me; for he said to me, Go not empty unto thy mother in law. [18] Then said she, Sit still, my daughter, until thou know how the matter will fall: for the man will not be in rest, until he have finished the thing this day" (Ruth 3:11-18).

Have you ever considered what is necessary before people consider something a miracle? We define a miracle as God supernaturally intervening and doing what man considers impossible. The more impossible something appears from the human perspective, the greater the miracle appears to be. The reality is it is no more difficult for God to do a miracle then it is for us to breathe.

"[26] Then came the word of the LORD unto Jeremiah, saying, [27] Behold, I *am* the LORD, the God of all flesh: is there any thing too hard for me" (Jeremiah 32:26-27)?

God's creation is a miracle to us because we cannot understand how God can create something from nothing. This is a *great* miracle to us simply because of its scope and magnitude.

However, creation is not a miracle to God. It was no more difficult or less difficult than anything else God does.

On one occasion Joshua prayed (Joshua 10:12-13) and asked God for more time to win the battle at Gibeon and time stopped for almost "one whole day." The Sun just stayed in the same place in the sky for about 24 hours. We look at that and say *that is a great miracle*.

On another occasion, Israel was leaving Egypt after four-hundred years of bondage while fleeing from the pursuing armies of Pharaoh (the most powerful army in the world at that time). God opened the Red Sea, dried the ground under the feet of three million people to pass through safely only to watch as God closed the same waters upon the army of Pharaoh drowning them. We look at that and say *that is a great miracle*.

When Israel came to the Promised Land after wandering in the wilderness for forty years, they came to the Jordan River, swollen and at flood stage (Joshua 3:15). When the feet of the priests stepped into the flood waters of the Jordan as God directed them to do, the waters retreated and stood in a wall twenty-one miles upriver almost to the city of Adam (Joshua 3:15). We look at that and say *that is a great miracle*.

What is the greatest miracle in the Bible? The greatest miracle in the Bible is the redemption of fallen sinners by a Holy God. The greatest miracle ever recorded was when the Holy God of glory stepped into humanity through the womb of a woman. He did that to become a man to go to the Cross of Calvary and pay the wages of sin to redeem fallen humanity from the curse of death. The greatest, most incredible miracle in the Bible is the miracle of redemption.

When we think of redemption, seldom do we think of it as an extreme miracle. Neither do we consider the cost of our redemption to God. We talk of the *Cross of redemption*. We discuss the blood sacrifice of Jesus, His death, and resurrection. However, do we really stop to think of the enormous sacrifice God made in order to accomplish our redemption? Read Psalm 49:6-7 and 9 (reading verse 8 after verse 9).

"[6] They that trust in their wealth, and boast themselves in the multitude of their riches; [7] None *of them* can by any means redeem his brother, nor give to God a ransom for him: [8] (For the redemption of their soul *is* precious, and it ceaseth for ever:) [9] That he should still live for ever, *and* not see corruption" (Psalm 49:6-9).

If a man completely possessed the accumulative wealth of the whole earth, it would not be enough to pay the price of redemption of just one lost soul (vs. 6-7). Real redemption not only removes us from the condemnation of sin and fallen creation, but it restores us to the original, perfect, and sinless specifications of the original creation in the Lord Jesus Christ (v. 9).

The word "precious" in Psalm 49:8 is from the Hebrew word *yaqar* (yaw-kar'). *Yaqar* refers to *the appraisal of something extremely valuable.* The reference is to the cost of redemption and the value God puts upon the human soul. God loves us to such an extreme that He was willing to go beyond the wealth of this world to pay the price of our redemption. He was willing to give Himself for our redemption.

> "Who gave himself for our sins, that he might deliver us from this present evil world, according to the will of God and our Father" (Galatians 1:4).

> "I am crucified with Christ: nevertheless I live; yet not I, but Christ liveth in me: and the life which I now live in the flesh I live by the faith of the Son of God, who loved me, and gave himself for me" (Galatians 2:20).

> "Husbands, love your wives, even as Christ also loved the church, and gave himself for it;" (Ephesians 5:25).

> "Who gave himself a ransom for all, to be testified in due time" (I Timothy 2:6).

> "Who gave himself for us, that he might redeem us from all iniquity, and purify unto himself a peculiar people, zealous of good works" (Titus 2:14).

When God paid the price of redemption for fallen humanity in the work of Jesus Christ, He went far beyond any miracle He had ever done before, even beyond the miracle of creation itself.

"⁵ Let this mind be in you, which was also in Christ Jesus: ⁶ Who, being in the form of God, thought it not robbery to be equal with God: ⁷ But made himself of no reputation, and took upon him the form of a servant, and was made in the likeness of men: ⁸ And being found in fashion as a man, he humbled himself, and became obedient unto death, even the death of the cross" (Philippians 2:5-8).

While we read these words, can we really understand their significance? The one, only, eternal, holy, omnipotent, omnipresent, omniscient, Creator God stepped out of the glories of heaven (the glory He created by His presence). He then stepped into this fallen creation by becoming a man and putting on a body of flesh with the sole purpose of righteously paying the death sentence that He put upon humanity. He did this just so people (like each of us who have rebelled against Him from the beginning) could be redeemed. The Creator humbled Himself before His own creatures and died in their place.

We hear of that enormous overwhelming love for us and set with stoic faces and hard hearts complaining about coming to church on Sunday. I hear people complain about the demands on their time to serve the Lord. I think the greatest miracle of the Bible is not that God was able to redeem, but that He was willing to redeem us.

"For the man will not be in rest, until he have finished the thing this day" (Ruth 3:18b). From the moment of the fall of man into sin, God has been preoccupied with redemption and man's restoration to stand in His grace (Romans 5:2). In John 4:32-34 (the Samaritan woman), Christ had sent His disciples (all of them) into the city to buy food (John 4:8). When they returned, they offered Him some to which He replied, "I have to eat that ye know not of."

"³² But he said unto them, I have meat to eat that ye know not of. ³³ Therefore said the disciples one to another, Hath any man brought him *ought* to eat? ³⁴ Jesus saith unto them, My meat is to do the will of him that sent me, and to finish his work" (John 4:32-34).

His disciples began to question each other about who had given Him food to eat. To which Christ answers, "My meat is to do the will of Him that sent me, and to finish His work." The unfinished work was the work of our redemption. He would not rest until the work of our redemption was finished. Everything else was just a prelude to that.

"But Jesus answered them, My Father worketh hitherto, and I work" (John 5:17).

"[24] Verily, verily, I say unto you, He that heareth my word, and believeth on him that sent me, hath everlasting life, and shall not come into condemnation; but is passed from death unto life. [25] Verily, verily, I say unto you, The hour is coming, and now is, when the dead shall hear the voice of the Son of God: and they that hear shall live. [26] For as the Father hath life in himself; so hath he given to the Son to have life in himself; [27] And hath given him authority to execute judgment also, because he is the Son of man. [28] Marvel not at this: for the hour is coming, in the which all that are in the graves shall hear his voice, [29] And shall come forth; they that have done good, unto the resurrection of life; and they that have done evil, unto the resurrection of damnation" (John 5:24-29).

According to John 5:17, both the Father and the Son would never cease working until the work of redemption was finally complete. According to John 5:24-29, until the work of redemption was complete, no one could pass "from death unto life" (referring to eternity as the New Creation).

"[28] After this, Jesus knowing that all things were now accomplished, that the scripture might be fulfilled, saith, I thirst. [29] Now there was set a vessel full of vinegar: and they filled a spunge with vinegar, and put *it* upon hyssop, and put *it* to his mouth. [30] When Jesus therefore had received the vinegar, he said, It is finished: and he bowed his head, and gave up the ghost" (John 19:28-30).

"It is finished." Say that aloud. The work of redemption is finished. Amen! Sing glory to God! Redemption is not finished in the waters of baptism. Redemption is not finished by you speaking in some *ecstatic language*. Redemption is not finished by your good works or by your participation in some religious ritual or ceremony. Your redemption was finished by the shedding of the blood of Jesus Christ and His substitutionary death on the Cross of Calvary two-thousand years ago.

"[18] Forasmuch as ye know that ye were not redeemed with corruptible things, *as* silver and gold, from your vain conversation *received* by tradition from your fathers; [19] But with the precious blood of Christ, as of a lamb without blemish and without spot: [20]

Who verily was foreordained before the foundation of the world, but was manifest in these last times for you, ²¹ Who by him do believe in God, that raised him up from the dead, and gave him glory; <u>that your faith and hope might be in God</u>" (I Peter 1:18-21).

Handfuls On Purpose
Studies in the Book of Ruth
Chapter Seventeen
The Miracle of Redemption

Three Requirements of a Redeemer

- ➢ He must be <u>able</u> to redeem.
- ➢ He must be <u>willing</u> to redeem.
- ➢ He must have the <u>right</u> to redeem.

1. Define what constitutes a miracle.

2. Discuss some of the miracles mentioned in this lesson. Discuss why we consider them to be *great* miracles.

3. Discuss why redemption is the greatest miracle in the Bible.

4. Explain Psalm 49:6-9 and discuss the cost of redemption.

5. Read Philippians 2:5-8 and discuss the statement, "When God redeemed fallen mankind in the work of Jesus Christ, He went far beyond any miracle He had ever done before, even beyond the miracle of creation itself."

6. Read John 4:32-34 with Ruth 3:18. According to John 4:34, what are the two things with which Jesus was preoccupied?

7. Read John 5:17 and 24-29. Explain these verses in the light of the doctrine of redemption.

8. Read John 19:28-30. When Jesus said, "It is finished," what was finished? What does "it is finished" mean? What practices of *Christianity* are excluded by the words "it is finished"?

9. Explain I Peter 1:18-21 from the context of your answer in the previous question.

Handfuls On Purpose
Studies in the Book of Ruth
Chapter Eighteen
The Redeemer That Cannot Redeem

"¹ Then went Boaz up to the gate, and sat him down there: and, behold, the kinsman of whom Boaz spake came by; unto whom he said, Ho, such a one! turn aside, sit down here. And he turned aside, and sat down. ² And he took ten men of the elders of the city, and said, Sit ye down here. And they sat down. ³ And he said unto the kinsman, Naomi, that is come again out of the country of Moab, selleth a parcel of land, which *was* our brother Elimelech's: ⁴ And I thought to advertise thee, saying, Buy *it* before the inhabitants, and before the elders of my people. If thou wilt redeem *it*, redeem *it*: but if thou wilt not redeem *it, then* tell me, that I may know: for *there is* none to redeem *it* beside thee; and I *am* after thee. And he said, I will redeem *it*. ⁵ Then said Boaz, What day thou buyest the field of the hand of Naomi, thou must buy *it* also of Ruth the Moabitess, the wife of the dead, to raise up the name of the dead upon his inheritance. ⁶ And the kinsman said, I cannot redeem *it* for myself, lest I mar mine own inheritance: redeem thou my right to thyself; for I cannot redeem *it*" (Ruth 4:1-6).

If we were to ask most people why they think they will go to Heaven when they die, they will answer that they have tried to do the best they could. There are millions of people, all over this world, who have been deceived into believing they will go to Heaven because they have done their best in trying to keep the Ten Commandments. Most of these people are just doing whatever someone told them they had to do. They believed what some *authority* told them because they thought that *authority* had a degree of expertise in his field. How important is it for people to understand that keeping the Law cannot save?

Most of these people are sincere people. They want to do what is right. Nonetheless, someone has misled them. These people work very hard at being moral people with the hope that one day they will have done enough good to outweigh the sins they may have committed or forgotten to confess. They think they will one day come before *St. Peter* in Heaven and he will put their good works on one side of the scales and their sins on the other side. If the good outweighs the bad, the *Pearly Gates* will open for them. If not, a *trap door* will open and they will fall into purgatory for a few million years. Christ said many would come to Him at the Day of Judgment claiming to have done the works necessary to be saved. He also tells us what His answer will be.

> "[22] Many will say to me in that day, Lord, Lord, have we not prophesied in thy name? and in thy name have cast out devils? and in thy name done many wonderful works? [23] And then will I profess unto them, I never knew you: depart from me, ye that work iniquity" (Matthew 7:22-23).

We should pity these people. It should be our hearts' greatest desire to see them escape their deception and come to know the truth of God's Word about what they need to do to be saved and go to Heaven. The only way that can happen is to teach them the real purpose of the Law and to help them understand the truth of the Gospel of Jesus Christ.

Again, the types in the book of Ruth are important. Boaz is a type of Christ. Ruth is a type of the Church. Naomi is a type of Israel. Now we are introduced to another type in the unnamed *kinsman redeemer*. He is a type of the Law as manifested by the twice-repeated words "I cannot redeem" in Ruth 4:6. The Law cannot redeem. Never forget those words. If the Law cannot redeem, keeping the Law cannot redeem a person.

The city gate was the courthouse of this period of history (Ruth 4:1). Boaz goes to the gate of the city and waits for the nearer *kinsman* to pass by. He calls the nearer *kinsma*n to sit down near him at the city gate for the purpose of settling a legal matter (4:1). He then calls together ten of the elders of the city to bear witness to the transaction and to offer legal opinion regarding Jewish Law, if necessary. Elders were usually men of age, well known in the community, spiritually mature, and considered to have wisdom in these types of decisions.

In Ruth 4:3-4, Boaz states his case and confronts this nearer kinsman with his moral obligations under the Law. In a small community like Bethlehem, this nearer kinsman would have known that Naomi had returned and that her husband and sons were dead. He should have fulfilled his responsibilities regarding this matter long ago, but did not. Instead, he allowed Naomi and Ruth to live in poverty and shame rather than show compassion and mercy on them.

The nearer kinsman was willing and able to redeem the land for Naomi. Then Boaz informs him there is more than the property in question (I cannot imagine that this nearer kinsman did not know this). There was the issue of this Gentile (Moabite) wife of the dead Mahlon who would need redemption with the land (Ruth 4:5).

Boaz is stating a legal point in that if the kinsman redeemer was going to redeem the property, he would also bear the responsibility of marrying Ruth with the intent of providing Elimelech and his son Mahlon a namesake. Read Ruth 4:6 again - "And the kinsman said, I cannot redeem *it* for myself, lest I mar mine own inheritance: redeem thou my right to thyself; for I cannot redeem *it.*" Why was the redemption of Ruth such a problem for this nearer kinsman as typical of the Law?

> "[3] An Ammonite or Moabite shall not enter into the congregation of the LORD; even to their tenth generation shall they not enter into the congregation of the LORD for ever: [4] Because they met you not with bread and with water in the way, when ye came forth out of Egypt; and because they hired against thee Balaam the son of Beor of Pethor of Mesopotamia, to curse thee" (Deuteronomy 23:3-4).

God put this restriction upon the Ammonites and Moabites due to their treachery in using a prophet of God against God's people. This incident with Ruth was less than one-hundred years after the event with Balaam. Ruth was a Moabite. The Law had no place, no time, no want, no welcome, and no concern for such a person. Ruth represents every person who has broken the Law. The Law simply acts in justice. There is no mercy, no love, and no grace. The Law shouts out in a trumpet voice, "The soul that sinneth, it shall die."

God's grace whispers in a still small voice, "He that believeth on Jesus hath everlasting life, and shall not come into judgment, but is passed from death unto life." Unlike Boaz as a type of Christ, the Law has no ability to love. However, God's love met the Law on the Cross of Calvary and God's love satisfied the Law's condemnation of all sin through the substitutionary death of Jesus Christ for all mankind (John 3:16). He took our death sentence and died in our place for our sin.

"²³ Who, when he was reviled, reviled not again; when he suffered, he threatened not; but committed *himself* to him that judgeth righteously: ²⁴ Who his own self bare our sins in his own body on the tree, that we, being dead to sins, should live unto righteousness: by whose stripes ye were healed" (I Peter 2:23-24).

"For Christ also hath once suffered for sins, the just for the unjust, that he might bring us to God, being put to death in the flesh, but quickened by the Spirit:" (I Peter 3:18).

Everyone needs to know and understand that the Law has no power to redeem. The Law takes the sinner by the hand and leads him to Christ, because it is powerless to redeem. Only the Gospel has power to redeem (Romans 1:16-17).

"¹⁰ For as many as are of the works of the law are under the curse: for it is written, Cursed *is* every one that continueth not in all things which are written in the book of the law to do them. ¹¹ But that no man is justified by the law in the sight of God, *it is* evident: for, The just shall live by faith. ¹² And the law is not of faith: but, The man that doeth them shall live in them. ¹³ Christ hath redeemed us from the curse of the law, being made a curse for us: for it is written, Cursed *is* every one that hangeth on a tree:" (Galatians 3:10-13).

"²¹ *Is* the law then against the promises of God? God forbid: for if there had been a law given which could have given life, verily righteousness should have been by the law. ²² But the scripture hath concluded all under sin, that the promise by faith of Jesus Christ might be given to them that believe. ²³ But before faith came, we were kept under the law, shut up unto the faith which should afterwards be revealed. ²⁴ Wherefore the law was our schoolmaster *to bring us* unto Christ, that we might be justified by faith" (Galatians 3:21-24).

People need to know that *any* attempt to earn salvation by Law keeping is an insult against the holiness of God, which demands absolute perfection and perfect righteousness.

"⁴ Christ is become of no effect unto you, whosoever of you are justified by the law; ye are fallen from grace. ⁵ For we through the Spirit wait for the hope of righteousness by faith. ⁶ For in Jesus Christ neither circumcision availeth any thing, nor uncircumcision;

but faith which worketh by love. ⁷ Ye did run well; who did hinder you that ye should not obey the truth? ⁸ This persuasion *cometh* not of him that calleth you. ⁹ A little leaven leaveneth the whole lump" (Galatians 5:4-9).

If anyone could achieve perfect righteousness by keeping commandments, why would God send His Son to die?

"I do not frustrate the grace of God: for if righteousness *come* by the law, then Christ is dead in vain" (Galatians 2:21).

The Gospels cannot possible be rendered in such a way that would allow anyone to come up with a theology that says there is salvation by keeping the Law. You cannot read the epistle to Romans and come up with a theology that says there is salvation by keeping the Law and you definitely cannot read the epistle to the Hebrews and come up with that kind of belief. You absolutely cannot read the epistle to the Galatians and come up with a theology that says there is salvation by keeping the Law.

This redundancy is to establish this theological precedent for why the *nearer kinsman* (as typical of the Law) of Ruth 4:1-6 says "I cannot redeem." Just as we have already read in Galatians 3:10, the Law cannot save anyone. All the Law does is curse the guilty.

"[19] Now we know that what things soever the law saith, it saith to them who are under the law: that every mouth may be stopped, and all the world may become guilty before God. [20] Therefore by the deeds of the law there shall no flesh be justified in his sight: for by the law *is* the knowledge of sin" (Romans 3:19-20).

We are all guilty (Romans 3:23) and the death sentence is upon every one of us (Romans 6:23).

"For whosoever shall keep the whole law, and yet offend in one *point*, he is guilty of all" (James 2:10).

The Law cannot redeem. Telling people that the Law cannot redeem is as much a part of the Gospel as is the death, burial, and resurrection of Christ. That is why the epistle to the Romans spends three and a half chapters dealing with this issue BEFORE we are given the details of the death, burial, and resurrection of Christ. The sinner MUST understand that the only thing he can do as he stands before the Law is to plead guilty. In knowing that reality, the only avenue before the sinner is to plead for mercy and grace.

Handfuls On Purpose
Studies in the Book of Ruth
Chapter Eighteen
The Redeemer That Cannot Redeem

1. Why do most people in the American society expect to go to Heaven?

2. If people are honestly trying their best to keep the commandments, will they be immoral or wicked people?

3. Read Matthew 7:22-23. What is Christ's pre-recorded answer (and therefore warning) to people thinking they will get into Heaven based upon keeping the Law or doing good works?

4. Why is it so important to understand that the only hope for lost people, trusting in their *works* or *rituals,* is to have someone who loves them enough to tell them the truth and teach them what Jesus has done to save them (the Gospel)?

5. What is the unnamed kinsman redeemer a type of in Ruth 4:1-6?

6. What is the all-conclusive statement of the Law regarding the redemption of a lost sinner in Ruth 4:6?

7. Thoroughly discuss this whole scene at the city gate of Bethlehem from the historical context of the book of Ruth.

8. Read Deuteronomy 23:3-4. Discuss why the *nearer kinsman* as typical of the Law could redeem the land, but not Ruth.

9. Read John 3:16, I Peter 2:23-24, and 3:18. Discuss how God's love changes this equation - sin equals condemnation.

10. Read Galatians 3:10-13 and 21-24. Discuss why it is so important that people understand that the Law has absolutely no power to redeem.

11. Read Galatians 5:4-9 and 2:21. Expand upon your above answer.

12. Read Romans 3:19-20 and James 2:10. Discuss the true message of the Law to all humanity.

13. The word *repent* means *to change the mind* or *to turn from one course of action to another*. How does this meaning relate to those who believe in salvation by works?

Handfuls On Purpose
Studies in the Book of Ruth
Chapter Nineteen
The Shoeless Redeemer

"⁷ Now this *was the manner* in former time in Israel concerning redeeming and concerning changing, for to confirm all things; a man plucked off his shoe, and gave *it* to his neighbour: and this *was* a testimony in Israel. ⁸ Therefore the kinsman said unto Boaz, Buy *it* for thee. So he drew off his shoe. ⁹ And Boaz said unto the elders, and *unto* all the people, Ye *are* witnesses this day, that I have bought all that *was* Elimelech's, and all that *was* Chilion's and Mahlon's, of the hand of Naomi. ¹⁰ Moreover Ruth the Moabitess, the wife of Mahlon, have I purchased to be my wife, to raise up the name of the dead upon his inheritance, that the name of the dead be not cut off from among his brethren, and from the gate of his place: ye *are* witnesses this day. ¹¹ And all the people that *were* in the gate, and the elders, said, *We are* witnesses. The LORD make the woman that is come into thine house like Rachel and like Leah, which two did build the house of Israel: and do thou {*get thee riches, or power*} worthily in Ephratah, and be famous {*proclaim thy name*} in Bethlehem: ¹² And let thy house be like the house of Pharez, whom Tamar bare unto Judah, of the seed which the LORD shall give thee of this young woman" (Ruth 4:7-12).

The word "kinsman" (Ruth 4:1) is from the Hebrew word *ga'al* (gaw-al'). It is a broad term covering a wide range of responsibilities. The *kinsman redeemer* had three basic obligations.

1. If poverty had compelled his brother (or family member) to sell his land or himself to be someone's bond slave, the *kinsman* was morally obligated (if he had the ability to do so) to buy back the land and/or pay the price to free his brother/relative from slavery.
2. The *kinsman* was also morally obligated to avenge the murder of his brother.
3. Lastly, if he was able, he was responsible to marry his dead brother's wife and raise up a successor to his brother's name if that brother died without leaving a son. In the case of Ruth and Naomi, this was true of both Elimelech and Mahlon (Ruth's dead husband).

If he was able to marry his brother's wife, but refused to raise up a successor to his brother's name, the Law had specific instructions about what the widow should do. In the case of the unnamed *kinsman*, it was not that he *would not*, but that he *could not* redeem Ruth.

> "[5] If brethren dwell together {*detailing they shared an inheritance*}, and one of them die, and have no child, the wife of the dead shall not marry without unto a stranger: her husband's brother {*or, her next kinsman*} shall go in unto her, and take her to him to wife, and perform the duty of an husband's brother unto her. [6] And it shall be, *that* the firstborn which she beareth shall succeed in the name of his brother *which is* dead, that his name be not put out of Israel. [7] And if the man like not to take his brother's wife, then let his brother's wife go up to the gate unto the elders, and say, My husband's brother refuseth to raise up unto his brother a name in Israel, he will not perform the duty of my husband's brother [8] Then the elders of his city shall call him, and speak unto him: and *if* he stand *to it*, and say, I like not to take her; [9] Then shall his brother's wife come unto him in the presence of the elders, and loose his shoe from off his foot, and spit in his face, and shall answer and say, So shall it be done unto that man that will not build up his brother's house. [10] And his name shall be called in Israel, The house of him that hath his shoe loosed" (Deuteronomy 25:5-10).

Since the unnamed *kinsman* (the Law) could not redeem, he relinquishes all claims of redemption. The unnamed kinsman signifies this by giving his shoe to Boaz (Ruth 4:7). In the physical sense, redemption involved removing a person from a place of insecurity and struggles to a place of security and rest. In the spiritual sense, redemption is the release from the bondage of sin *and* from the fear of the death sentence upon all sinners.

Therefore, in the spiritual sense, redemption releases a person from the fear of condemnation and death (Hell) and delivers him to a place of security in Christ ("rest") with the hope of resurrection and glorification. The Law pronounces all men guilty of sin and puts us in bondage to the constant fear of death (eternal separation from God). This is why the Law cannot redeem lost souls. The Law pronounces all men guilty of sin, condemns them to death, and puts them in bondage on death row awaiting the day of their execution. When Christ redeems us, it is a complete and absolute deliverance.

"And deliver them who through fear of death were all their lifetime subject to bondage" (Hebrews 2:15).

"Christ hath redeemed us from the curse of the law, being made a curse for us: for it is written, Cursed *is* every one that hangeth on a tree:" (Galatians 3:13).

The Law could not redeem because it was the Law that cursed the sinner. When the unnamed kinsman (the Law) gives his shoe to Boaz (a type of Christ), he relinquishes all claims on the sinner, including the curse. The shoe represents the curse of the Law in the handwriting of the ordinances of the Law that testify against us.

Get this visual picture, Christ took the Law's "shoe" (the handwriting of ordinances against the sinner) and nailed it to the Cross, paying its penalty for all sinners (Colossians 2:14). If the believer has truly been redeemed and "born again," his redemption (salvation) is positionally complete *in* Christ. All that has happened to Christ has happened to the believer positionally.

"[9] For in him dwelleth all the fulness of the Godhead bodily. [10] And ye are complete in him, which is the head of all principality and power: [11] In whom also ye are circumcised with the circumcision made without hands, in putting off the body of the sins of the flesh by the circumcision of Christ: [12] Buried with him in baptism, wherein also ye are risen with *him* through the faith of the operation of God, who hath raised him from the dead. [13] And you, being dead in your sins and the uncircumcision of your flesh, hath he quickened together with him, having forgiven you all trespasses; [14] Blotting out the handwriting of ordinances that was against us, which was contrary to us, and took it out of the way, nailing it to his cross; [15] *And* having spoiled principalities and powers, he made a shew of them openly, triumphing over them in it" (Colossians 2:9-15).

Christ presents the redeemed believer to God "holy and unblameable and unreprovable" (Colossians 1:22).

"[20] And, having made peace through the blood of his cross, by him to reconcile all things unto himself; by him, *I say*, whether *they be* things in earth, or things in heaven. [21] And you, that were sometime alienated and enemies in *your* mind by wicked works, yet now hath he reconciled [22] In the body of his flesh through death, to present you holy and unblameable and unreproveable in his sight: [23] If ye continue in the faith grounded and settled, and *be* not moved away from the hope of the gospel, which ye have heard, *and* which was preached to every creature which is under heaven; whereof I Paul am made a minister;" (Colossians 1:20-23).

"Holy" is from the Greek word *hagios* (hag'-ee-os), referring to something or someone set apart for God. It means that Christ has presented us as Saints in the "sight" of God. "Unblameable" is from the Greek word *amomos* (am'-o-mos), which signifies He presents the believing sinner to God morally faultless and perfectly cleansed. "Unreprovable" is from the Greek word *anegkletos* (an-eng'-klay-tos), which means Christ presents the believing sinner unaccusable before God as one who cannot be called into account for sin. The only condition (Colossians 1:23) is that the sinner continue trusting in Christ to save him. Since faith is a product of enabling grace, it is the indwelling Holy Spirit who will enable the true "born again" believer to "continue" trusting his soul into the care of Christ.

In the redemption of Ruth, Naomi is also redeemed (Ruth 4:10). These two women together represent the Church as being a construct of both Jew and Gentile. Ruth was a Gentile. Naomi was a Jew. In Christ the Redeemer, the two are made one through faith and together make up the Church.

"[11] Wherefore remember, that ye *being* in time past Gentiles in the flesh, who are called Uncircumcision by that which is called the Circumcision in the flesh made by hands; [12] That at that time ye were without Christ, being aliens from the commonwealth of Israel, and strangers from the covenants of promise, having no hope, and without God in the world: [13] But now in Christ Jesus ye who sometimes were far off are made nigh by the blood of Christ. [14] For he is our peace, who hath made both one, and hath broken down the middle wall of partition *between us*; [15] Having abolished in his flesh the enmity, *even* the law of commandments *contained* in ordinances; for to make in himself of twain one new man, *so* making peace; [16] And that he might reconcile both unto God in one body by the cross, having slain the enmity thereby: [17] And came and preached peace to you which were afar off, and to them that were nigh. [18] For through him we both have access by one Spirit unto the

Father. ¹⁹ Now therefore ye are no more strangers and foreigners, but fellowcitizens with the saints, and of the household of God; ²⁰ And are built upon the foundation of the apostles and prophets, Jesus Christ himself being the chief corner *stone*; ²¹ In whom all the building fitly framed together groweth unto an holy temple in the Lord: ²² In whom ye also are builded together for an habitation of God through the Spirit" (Ephesians 2:11-22).

Boaz was the son of Salmon and Rahab, the saved harlot of Jericho (Ruth 4:21).

"And Salmon begat Booz of Rachab; and Booz begat Obed of Ruth; and Obed begat Jesse;" (Matthew 1:5).

The significance of this is that Jesus was born of this line. Rahab and Ruth were Gentiles. There are both Gentiles and Jews in Christ's genealogy. Therefore, He is the *kinsman* of both Jew and Gentile and can redeem both equally.

"²¹ But now the righteousness of God without the law is manifested, being witnessed by the law and the prophets; ²² Even the righteousness of God *which is* by faith of Jesus Christ unto all and upon all them that believe: for there is no difference:" (Romans 3:21-22).

"²⁸ Therefore we conclude that a man is justified by faith without the deeds of the law. ²⁹ *Is he* the God of the Jews only? *is he* not also of the Gentiles? Yes, of the Gentiles also: ³⁰ Seeing *it is* one God, which shall justify the circumcision by faith, and uncircumcision through faith" (Romans 3:28-30).

This is the context of the "whosoever" of Romans 10:13.

"⁹ That if thou shalt confess with thy mouth the Lord Jesus, and shalt believe in thine heart that God hath raised him from the dead, thou shalt be saved. ¹⁰ For with the heart man believeth unto righteousness; and with the mouth confession is made unto salvation. ¹¹ For the scripture saith, Whosoever believeth on him shall not be ashamed. ¹² For there is no difference between the Jew and the Greek: for the same Lord over all is rich unto all that call upon him. ¹³ For whosoever shall call upon the name of the Lord shall be saved" (Romans 10:9-13).

Handfuls On Purpose
Studies in the Book of Ruth
Chapter Nineteen
The Shoeless Redeemer

1. List and explain the three basic obligations of a *kinsman redeemer*.

2. Discuss the significance of the difference between the *would not* and the *could not* of the unnamed *kinsman redeemer's* ability to redeem Ruth.

3. Read Deuteronomy 25:5-10 and explain the reason why the unnamed *nearer kinsman* took off his shoe and gave it to Boaz (Ruth 4:7-8). Explain why Ruth was not there and does not "spit in his face" (v. 9 - consider your answer to question two regarding the latter).

4. Discuss the differences between the physical aspect of redemption under the Law and the spiritual realities it typified.

5. When Christ redeems the believing sinner, it is a complete and absolute deliverance. Explain how the following verses relate that truth.
   A. Hebrews 2:15:
   B. Galatians 3:13:

6. Read Colossians 1:20-23 and explain the following terms as they relate to a believer's redemption.
   A. "Holy"
   B. "Unblameable"
   C. "Unreprovable"

7. Read Colossians 2:9-15 and discuss the significance of the words "ye are complete <u>in</u> Him" as they relate to a believer's redemption <u>in</u> Christ Jesus.

8. Discuss the significance of the fact that Naomi's redemption is wrapped up in Ruth's redemption as it relates to the Church as a spiritual entity.

9. Read Matthew 1:5, Romans 3:21-22, 28-30 and 10:9-13. Discuss the significance of the fact that Boaz was the son of Rahab (a saved Gentile) and both are in the genealogy of Christ.

10. From the context of your above answer, discuss the "whosoever will" of Romans 10:13.

Handfuls On Purpose
Studies in the Book of Ruth
Chapter Twenty
"That the Name of the Dead be Not Cut Off"

"⁹ And Boaz said unto the elders, and *unto* all the people, Ye *are* witnesses this day, that I have bought all that *was* Elimelech's, and all that *was* Chilion's and Mahlon's, of the hand of Naomi. ¹⁰ Moreover Ruth the Moabitess, the wife of Mahlon, have I purchased to be my wife, to raise up the name of the dead upon his inheritance, that the name of the dead be not cut off from among his brethren, and from the gate of his place: ye *are* witnesses this day" (Ruth 4:9-10).

The children of God are responsible to tell others of His wonderful works in the lives of people. If they will not tell others, who will? Whatever God does in lives, He expects those same people to proclaim those things to everyone simply because of how wonderful and gracious God is.

"¹ O give thanks unto the LORD; call upon his name: make known his deeds among the people. ² Sing unto him, sing psalms unto him: talk ye of all his wondrous works. ³ Glory ye in his holy name: let the heart of them rejoice that seek the LORD. ⁴ Seek the LORD, and his strength: seek his face evermore. ⁵ Remember his marvellous works that he hath done; his wonders, and the judgments of his mouth; ⁶ O ye seed of Abraham his servant, ye children of Jacob his chosen. ⁷ He *is* the LORD our God: his judgments *are* in all the earth" (Psalm 105:1-7).

The word "witnesses" in Ruth 4:9 is from the Hebrew word `ed (ayd), meaning to see and give testimony to the facts. It is contracted from the root word `uwd (ood), meaning to repeat, bear witness, or to say again and again. In other words, the witnesses to this transaction were responsible to insure that everyone heard of this transaction, and from that day forward, accept and treat Ruth as Boaz's wife.

These witnesses were commanded to talk about this with everyone they met. Uniquely, that is a literal meaning of the Great Commission of Christ to His disciples. It might read, *"As you are going along your everyday walk of life, talk about Me and what I have done to redeem lost souls from the bondage of sin and death (the Gospel). Tell everyone. See that this message is broadcast throughout the whole world."*

Yet, many people, who profess to be born again, have told no one of the wonderful gift of redemption that God has given them. They have not even told their neighbors of the God who loves us all. They never speak of the love of God that sent His only begotten Son into the world to become a man to go to the Cross and take our death sentence. They never explain that Jesus came to pay our sin debt for us. Many professing Christians have never shared the wonders of salvation and the truths of the Gospel with anyone. Yet they have the gall to call themselves Christians and claim to be the children of God.

The central work of the ministry given to all Christians by the Lord is making known what God has done and is going to do. This message centers upon the doctrine of redemption. However, redemption goes beyond the redemption of lost souls. Therefore, God commands all Christians to proclaim the message of redemption. That message involves both what Christ has done in His first advent and what He will do in His second advent. The purpose of the second coming of Christ will be to bless His redeemed and remove them from the dominion of the "prince and power of the air" (Satan).

Satan's plot to steal the dominion of this world from Adam involved deceiving Eve. However, when Adam chose to sin rather than obey God, Adam lost dominion of this world to Satan. The whole creation (including man) came under the curse of God and required redemption. Adam's sin brought the curse of condemnation and death upon all of the first creation. The righteousness of Christ and His substitutionary death brought life, redemption, and reconciliation for all of God's creation.

Our redemption goes beyond the salvation of our souls. Our redemption involves an inheritance that is also ours in Christ.

> "[17] And if children, then heirs; heirs of God, and joint-heirs with Christ; if so be that we suffer with *him*, that we may be also glorified together. [18] For I reckon that the sufferings of this present time *are* not worthy *to be compared* with the glory which shall be revealed in us. [19] For the earnest expectation of the creature {*ktis'-is,*

referring to creation} waiteth for the manifestation of the sons of God *{referring to the glorification}*. [20] For the creature *{creation}* was made subject to vanity, not willingly, but by reason of him who hath subjected *the same* in hope, [21] Because the creature *{creation}* itself also shall be delivered from the bondage of corruption into the glorious liberty of the children of God. [22] For we know that the whole creation groaneth and travaileth in pain together until now. [23] And not only *they*, but ourselves also, which have the firstfruits of the Spirit, even we ourselves groan within ourselves, waiting for the adoption, *to wit*, the redemption of our body" (Romans 8:17-23).

When believers are regenerated ("born again"), they become the children of God. All truly "born again" Christians will share in Christ's dominion over creation when they are glorified (at the rapture) and return with Christ at His second coming to rule with Him over the earth.

"[26] And he that overcometh, and keepeth my works unto the end, to him will I give power over the nations [27] And he shall rule them with a rod of iron; as the vessels of a potter shall they be broken to shivers: even as I received of my Father [28] And I will give him the morning star *{probably refers to the believer's glorification}*" (Revelation 2:26-28).

Jesus is coming again. This is not science fiction. This is theological fact and a sure future reality. When Jesus returns, He will not be coming as the meek and lowly Savior. He will be the glorified God/man coming in *power* and in *fierce judgment*.

"[12] And I turned to see the voice that spake with me. And being turned, I saw seven golden candlesticks; [13] And in the midst of the seven candlesticks *one* like unto the Son of man, clothed with a garment down to the foot, and girt about the paps with a golden girdle. [14] His head and *his* hairs *were* white like wool, as white as snow; and his eyes *were* as a flame of fire; [15] And his feet like unto fine brass, as if they burned in a furnace; and his voice as the sound of many waters. [16] And he had in his right hand seven stars: and out of his mouth went a sharp twoedged sword: and his countenance *was* as the sun shineth in his strength. [17] And when I saw him, I fell at his feet as dead. And he laid his right hand upon me, saying unto me, Fear not; I am the first and the last: [18] I *am* he that liveth, and was dead; and, behold, I am alive for evermore, Amen; <u>and have the keys of hell and of death</u>" (Revelation 1:12-18).

"¹¹ And I saw heaven opened, and behold a white horse; and he that sat upon him *was* called Faithful and True, and in righteousness he doth judge and make war. ¹² His eyes *were* as a flame of fire, and on his head *were* many crowns; and he had a name written, that no man knew, but he himself. ¹³ And he *was* clothed with a vesture dipped in blood: and his name is called The Word of God. ¹⁴ And the armies *which were* in heaven followed him upon white horses, clothed in fine linen, white and clean. ¹⁵ <u>And out of his mouth goeth a sharp sword, that with it he should smite the nations: and he shall rule them with a rod of iron: and he treadeth the winepress of the fierceness and wrath of Almighty God. 16 And he hath on *his* vesture and on his thigh a name written, KING OF KINGS, AND LORD OF LORDS</u>" (Revelation 19:11-16).

When Jesus comes again, He will claim the dominion over the creation He has redeemed (Revelation 5:1-10).

"¹ And I saw in the right hand of him that sat on the throne a book written within and on the backside, sealed with seven seals. ² And I saw a strong angel proclaiming with a loud voice, <u>Who is worthy to open the book, and to loose the seals thereof?</u> ³ And no man in heaven, nor in earth, neither under the earth, was able to open the book, neither to look thereon. ⁴ And I wept much, because no man was found worthy to open and to read the book, neither to look thereon. ⁵ And one of the elders saith unto me, Weep not: behold, the Lion of the tribe of Juda, the Root of David, hath prevailed to open the book, and to loose the seven seals thereof. ⁶ And I beheld, and, lo, in the midst of the throne and of the four beasts, and in the midst of the elders, stood a Lamb as it had been slain, having seven horns and seven eyes, which are the seven Spirits of God {*see Isaiah 11:1-6 for an explanation of the meaning of this statement*} sent forth into all the earth. ⁷ And he came and took the book out of the right hand of him that sat upon the throne. ⁸ And when he had taken the book, the four beasts and four *and* twenty elders fell down before the Lamb, having every one of them harps, and golden vials full of **odours** {*incense*}, which are the prayers of saints. ⁹ <u>And they sung a new song, saying, Thou art worthy to take the book, and to open the seals thereof: for thou wast slain, and hast redeemed us to God by thy blood out of every kindred, and tongue, and people, and nation; ¹⁰ And hast made us unto our God kings and priests: and we shall reign on the earth</u>" (Revelation 5:1-10).

In first century, under Roman law, Romans used a seven-sealed scroll to transfer the title of assets of a deceased person to his heir. This "seven sealed scroll" is the *title deed* to the dominion over the entire earth.

Revelation 5:2 asks the question, "Who is worthy to open the book, and to loose the seals thereof?" Opening this scroll would require a man, but not just any man - it would require a perfect man. Opening this scroll would require a sinless man. According to Revelation 5:3, not one single human being was found who met the criteria necessary to lay claim to the title deed of dominion over the earth.

At the beginning of creation, God gave dominion over the earth to Adam.

> "And God said, Let us make man in our image, after our likeness: and let them have dominion over the fish of the sea, and over the fowl of the air, and over the cattle, and over all the earth, and over every creeping thing that creepeth upon the earth" (Genesis 1:26).

When Adam fell in sin, God cursed the earth itself.

> "And unto Adam he said, Because thou hast hearkened unto the voice of thy wife, and hast eaten of the tree, of which I commanded thee, saying, Thou shalt not eat of it: cursed *is* the ground for thy sake; in sorrow shalt thou eat *of* it all the days of thy life;" (Genesis 3:17).

Through the work of the cross, Christ (the last Adam, the God-man) won victory over the curse and purchased the possession of that dominion back through His redemption. When Christ finally takes this *title deed* of dominion over the earth, He will transpose His authority (dominion) to the Church during the Kingdom Age (the raptured and glorified New Covenant believers). The *title deed* of dominion over the earth is the Church's inheritance in the Kingdom.

> "[13] In whom ye also *trusted*, after that ye heard the word of truth, the gospel of your salvation: in whom also after that ye believed, ye were sealed with that holy Spirit of promise, [14] Which is the earnest of our inheritance until the redemption of the purchased possession, unto the praise of his glory" (Ephesians 1:13-14).

"[18] The eyes of your understanding being enlightened; that ye may know what is the hope of his calling, and what the riches of the glory of his inheritance in the saints, [19] And what *is* the exceeding greatness of his power to us-ward who believe, according to the working of his mighty power, [20] Which he wrought in Christ, when he raised him from the dead, and set *him* at his own right hand in the heavenly *places*, [21] Far above all principality, and power, and might, and dominion, and every name that is named, not only in this world, but also in that which is to come: [22] And hath put all *things* under his feet, and gave him *to be* the head over all *things* to the church, [23] Which is his body, the fulness of him that filleth all in all" (Ephesians 1:18-23).

Jesus the Redeemer is the "Lion of the tribe of Judah" and "the root of David" (Revelation 5:5). Both of these terms signify the lineage of the man who would be able to claim the *title deed* to the dominion over the earth. It is also a reminder of the coming Kingdom over which Messiah would rule on the throne of David. It is the Lord Jesus Christ, who will share His Kingdom rule with His Bride, the Church.

"Of the increase of *his* government and peace *there shall be* no end, upon the throne of David, and upon his kingdom, to order it, and to establish it with judgment and with justice from henceforth even for ever. The zeal of the LORD of hosts will perform this" (Isaiah 9:7).

After one of the "elders" asks John to "behold" the "lion of the tribe of Judah" and the "root of David," John turns to see (Revelation 5:6). However, John does not see what he expects to see. Instead John sees something else "in the midst of the throne" at the middle of this heavenly scene. He sees "a lamb as it had been slain." God uses the word "lamb," as used of the resurrected and glorified Jesus Christ, twenty-seven times in the book of Revelation. The use of the word "lamb" identifies and connects the redeemed with their Redeemer. It is by the means of His sacrifice at Calvary that He has "prevailed" to open the book and lay claim to the *title deed* of dominion over the earth for all the redeemed of mankind.

"[12] Wherefore, as by one man sin entered into the world, and death by sin; and so death passed upon all men, for that all have sinned: [13] (For until the law sin was in the world: but sin is not imputed when there is no law. [14] Nevertheless death reigned from Adam to Moses, even over them that had not sinned after the similitude of Adam's transgression, who is the figure of him that was to come. [15] But not as the offence, so also *is* the free gift. For if through the offence of one many be dead, much more the grace of God, and the gift by grace, *which is* by one man, Jesus Christ, hath abounded unto many. [16] And not as *it was* by one that sinned, *so is* the gift: for the judgment *was* by one to condemnation, but the free gift *is* of many offences unto justification. [17] <u>For if by one man's offence death reigned by one; much more they which receive abundance of grace and of the gift of righteousness shall reign in life by one, Jesus Christ</u>.) [18] Therefore as by the offence of one *judgment came* upon all men to condemnation; even so by the righteousness of one *the free gift came* upon all men unto justification of life. [19] For as by one man's disobedience many were made sinners, so by the obedience of one shall many be made righteous. [20] Moreover the law entered, that the offence might abound. But where sin abounded, grace did much more abound: [21] <u>That as sin hath reigned unto death, even so might grace reign through righteousness unto eternal life by Jesus Christ our Lord</u>" (Romans 5:12-21).

Handfuls On Purpose
Studies in the Book of Ruth
Chapter Twenty
"That the Name of the Dead be Not Cut Off"

1. Read Psalm 105:1-7 with Ruth 4:9. What is the foremost responsibility of "the elders, and . . . all the people" involving redemption?

2. Boaz redeemed both Ruth and the land. Discuss how this relates to the scope of redemption in Christ.

3. Read Romans 8:17-23. Discuss the meaning of this portion of Scripture from the context of your answer to question two.

4. Read Revelation 2:26-28. Discuss the believers' share in the redeemed dominion over the earth.

5. Read Revelation 1:12-18. Discuss the *word portrait* of Jesus Christ and what it reveals in the difference between His first advent and His second advent. Include the significance of the statement, "and have the keys of hell and of death" in your discussion.

6. Revelation 19:11-16 reveals the second coming of Christ to the earth. Discuss who the "armies" are that will follow Him in His second advent by comparing Revelation 2:26-28 with Revelation 19:14.

7. Read Revelation 5:1-10. Discuss the significance of the *seven-sealed* scroll as it regards the doctrine of redemption and the believer's inheritance in Christ.

8. Read Ephesians 1:13-14 and 18-23. Discuss what God means by the statement the Holy Spirit is His signature on His promise "of our inheritance until the redemption of the purchased possession." What is that inheritance?

9. According to Revelation 5:5, John saw Jesus as the "Lion of the tribe of Judah" and "the root of David." Discuss the significance of these terms as they relate to the doctrine of redemption.

10. Read Romans 5:12-21 and discuss the significance of the word "Lamb" as used in Revelation 5:6 to the doctrine of redemption.

Handfuls On Purpose
Studies in the Book of Ruth
Chapter Twenty-one
The Resurrection of the Bride of Christ

"[11] And all the people that *were* in the gate, and the elders, said, *We are* witnesses. The LORD make the woman that is come into thine house like Rachel and like Leah, which two did build the house of Israel: and do thou worthily in Ephratah, and be famous {*proclaim thy name*} in Bethlehem: [12] And let thy house be like the house of Pharez, whom Tamar bare unto Judah, of the seed which the LORD shall give thee of this young woman. [13] So Boaz took Ruth, and she was his wife: and when he went in unto her, the LORD gave her conception, and she bare a son" (Ruth 4:11-13).

Naomi represents saved Jews. Ruth represents saved Gentiles. Together they represent the Church made up of born again Jews and Gentiles. Just as Rachel and Leah built the "house of Israel, Naomi (saved Jews) and Ruth (saved Gentiles) will build *body of Christ* (His Church).

God does not reveal the span between Ruth 4:11-12 and the actual time of the marriage to us. It may have taken place immediately, or there may have been some time span involved. The picture before us is that of the Bride of Christ. Ruth 4:13 portrays the rapture of the Church and the Marriage Supper of the Lamb.

Oriental wedding customs follow the pattern of Scripture. An oriental marriage involved two stages: the *Kiddushin* (Betrothal) and the *Huppah* (Canopy; the bringing home of the bride). A Betrothal was considered a legally binding promise of marriage that afforded certain rights and privileges to the Bride. The woman, once betrothed, was considered and treated as a married woman. The betrothed woman was expected to be a virgin unless she was a widow. She was expected to remain a virgin until the *Huppah* ceremony. The time-period between the Betrothal and the *Huppah* could be days, months, or years in some cases.

When believing sinners accept Jesus Christ as Saviour and Lord, they become His betrothed. The believer has similar rights and privileges of a wife the moment he is saved. Once saved, all the redeemed await the coming of the Bridegroom for His Bride. The Bride is responsible to maintain her moral purity until the *Huppah*.

We know Christ's coming for His Bride theologically as the *rapture* of the Church.

"[15] For this we say unto you by the word of the Lord, that we which are alive *and* remain unto the coming of the Lord shall not prevent them which are asleep. [16] For the Lord himself shall descend from heaven with a shout, with the voice of the archangel, and with the trump of God: and the dead in Christ shall rise first: [17] Then we which are alive *and* remain shall be caught up together with them in the clouds, to meet the Lord in the air: and so shall we ever be with the Lord" (I Thessalonians 4:15-17).

The difference between the rapture and the second coming is that at the rapture Christ comes *for* His bride. At the second coming, Christ comes *with* His bride.

"To the end he may stablish your hearts unblameable in holiness before God, even our Father, at the coming of our Lord Jesus Christ with all his saints" (I Thessalonians 3:13).

The "witnesses" of Ruth 4:11 represent the witnesses to the proposal of redemption and marriage of Boaz (a type of Christ) to Ruth (along with Naomi, a type of the church). The resurrection of Jesus is the promise of the resurrection of the Church (redemption of our physical bodies) witnessed by hundreds of people. God summarizes this in I Corinthians 15:1-8.

"[1] Moreover, brethren, I declare unto you the gospel which I preached unto you, which also ye have received, and wherein ye stand; [2] By which also ye are saved, if ye keep in memory what I preached unto you, unless ye have believed in vain. [3] For I delivered unto you first of all that which I also received, how that Christ died for our sins according to the scriptures; [4] And that he was buried, and that he rose again the third day according to the scriptures: [5] And that he was seen of Cephas, then of the twelve: [6] After that, he was seen of above five hundred brethren at once; of whom the greater part remain unto this present, but some are fallen asleep. [7] After that, he was seen of James; then of all the apostles. [8] And last of all he was seen of me also, as of one born out of due time."

The taking home of the Bride usually involved a seven-day feast. This is typical of the Tribulation time. During these seven days, the Church will be in Heaven with Jesus during the "seventieth week of Daniel" on the earth (the seven-year tribulation). God calls this celebration in Heaven the Marriage Supper of the Lamb. We only need to read Revelation 19:6-9 to see the similarities to the statement of the witnesses in Ruth 4:11-12.

> "⁶ And I heard as it were the voice of a great multitude, and as the voice of many waters, and as the voice of mighty thunderings, saying, Alleluia: for the Lord God omnipotent reigneth. ⁷ Let us be glad and rejoice, and give honour to him: for the marriage of the Lamb is come, and his wife hath made herself ready. ⁸ And to her was granted that she should be arrayed in fine linen, clean and white: for the fine linen is the righteousness of saints. ⁹ And he saith unto me, Write, Blessed *are* they which are called unto the marriage supper of the Lamb. And he saith unto me, These are the true sayings of God" (Revelation 19:6-9).

The *Huppah* ceremony and the friends of the Bridegroom

The ceremony began with the bridegroom gathering all of his friends around him and going to the bride's home to take her for his wife. The redeemed of all ages are the friends of the Bridegroom as represented by John the Baptist.

> "²⁶ And they came unto John, and said unto him, Rabbi, he that was with thee beyond Jordan, to whom thou barest witness, behold, the same baptizeth, and all *men* come to him. ²⁷ John answered and said, A man can receive nothing, except it be given him from heaven. ²⁸ Ye yourselves bear me witness, that I said, I am not the Christ, but that I am sent before him. ²⁹ He that hath the bride is the bridegroom: but the friend of the bridegroom, which standeth and heareth him, rejoiceth greatly because of the bridegroom's voice: this my joy therefore is fulfilled. ³⁰ He must increase, but I *must* decrease" (John 3:26-30).

The united voice of all these redeemed souls, who are not part of the Church Age and who are around the throne of God, announce the Marriage Supper of the Lamb.

"⁶ And I heard as it were the voice of a great multitude, and as the voice of many waters, and as the voice of mighty thunderings, saying, Alleluia: for the Lord God omnipotent reigneth. ⁷ Let us be glad and rejoice, and give honour to him: for the marriage of the Lamb is come, and his wife hath made herself ready" (Revelation 19:6-7).

Finally, at the end of the celebration, the bride was escorted to the home of the bridegroom. This will take place at Christ's Second Advent, and is the next recorded event in Revelation 19:11-16.

The first resurrection/translation is in three phases.

God has already completed the first phase. This completion assures us of the next two phases. The first resurrection only involves those of the Church Age. Christ's resurrection is the "first fruit" of the first resurrection (I Thessalonians 4:14).

"²⁰ But now is Christ risen from the dead, and become the firstfruits of them that slept. ²¹ For since by man came death, by man came also the resurrection of the dead. ²² For as in Adam all die, even so in Christ shall all be made alive. ²³ But every man in his own order: Christ the firstfruits; afterward they that are Christ's at his coming" (I Corinthians 15:20-23).

The second phase of the first resurrection is the details of what God records in I Thessalonians 4:16-17, commonly referred to as the Rapture.

"⁵¹ Behold, I shew you a mystery; We shall not all sleep, but we shall all be changed, ⁵² In a moment, in the twinkling of an eye, at the last trump: for the trumpet shall sound, and the dead shall be raised incorruptible, and we shall be changed. ⁵³ For this corruptible must put on incorruption, and this mortal must put on immortality. ⁵⁴ So when this corruptible shall have put on incorruption, and this mortal shall have put on immortality, then shall be brought to pass the saying that is written, Death is swallowed up in victory" (I Corinthians 15:51-54).

The third phase of the first resurrection will take place after the seven-year tribulation period (exactly seven years after the second phase).

"¹ And I saw an angel come down from heaven, having the key of the bottomless pit and a great chain in his hand. ² And he laid hold on the dragon, that old serpent, which is the Devil, and Satan, and bound him a thousand years, ³ And cast him into the bottomless pit, and shut him up, and set a seal upon him, that he should deceive the nations no more, till the thousand years should be fulfilled: and after that he must be loosed a little season. ⁴ And I saw thrones, and they sat upon them, and judgment was given unto them: and I saw the souls of them that were beheaded for the witness of Jesus, and for the word of God, and which had not worshipped the beast, neither his image, neither had received his mark upon their foreheads, or in their hands; and they lived and reigned with Christ a thousand years. ⁵ But the rest of the dead lived not again until the thousand years were finished. <u>This is the first resurrection.</u> ⁶ Blessed and holy is he that hath part in the first resurrection: on such the second death hath no power, but they shall be priests of God and of Christ, and shall reign with him a thousand years" (Revelation 20:1-6).

This second resurrection will take place at the end of the Kingdom Age (one-thousand year reign of Christ on earth). This will involve all people from Adam to the end of the world, both saved and lost, who were not part of the first resurrection. Church Age people should be careful not to confuse these two different resurrections or the various phases of the first resurrection. For instance, Matthew 24:29-42 does not refer to the second phase of the first resurrection, but to the second coming of Christ just prior to the third phase.

"²⁹ <u>Immediately after the tribulation of those days</u> shall the sun be darkened, and the moon shall not give her light, and the stars shall fall from heaven, and the powers of the heavens shall be shaken: ³⁰ And then shall appear the sign of the Son of man in heaven: and then shall all the tribes of the earth mourn, and they shall see the Son of man coming in the clouds of heaven with power and great glory {*second coming, not the rapture*}. ³¹ And he shall send his angels with a great sound of a trumpet, and they shall gather together his elect from the four winds, from one end of heaven to the other {the rapture of the church}. ³² Now learn a parable of the fig tree; When his branch is yet tender, and putteth forth leaves, ye know that summer *is* nigh: ³³ So likewise ye, when ye shall see all these things, know that it is near, *even* at the doors. ³⁴ Verily I say unto you, This generation shall not pass, till all these things be fulfilled. [35] Heaven and earth shall pass away, but my words shall not pass away. [36] But of that day and hour knoweth no *man*, no, not the angels of heaven, but my Father only. [37] But as the days of Noe *were*, so shall also the coming of the Son of man be. [38] For as in the days that were before the flood they were eating and drinking, marrying and giving in marriage, until the day that Noe entered into the ark, [39] And knew not until the flood came, and took them all away; so shall also the coming of the Son of man be. [40] Then shall two be in the field; the one shall be taken, and the other left. [41] Two *women shall be* grinding at the mill; the one shall be taken, and the other left. [42] Watch therefore: for ye know not what hour your Lord doth come" (Matthew 24:29-42).

The parable of the separation of the tares from the wheat in Matthew 13:24-30 refers neither to the rapture nor to the second coming. It refers to the second resurrection just after the Millennial Kingdom and just before the Great White Throne Judgment (Revelation 20:7-15 and Daniel 12:1-3).

"[24] Another parable put he forth unto them, saying, The kingdom of heaven is likened unto a man which sowed good seed in his field: [25] But while men slept, his enemy came and sowed tares among the wheat, and went his way. [26] But when the blade was sprung up, and brought forth fruit, then appeared the tares also. [27] So the servants of the householder came and said unto him, Sir, didst not thou sow good seed in thy field? from whence then hath it tares? [28] He said unto them, An enemy hath done this. The servants said unto him, Wilt thou then that we go and gather them up? [29] But he said, Nay; lest while ye gather up the tares, ye root up also the wheat with them. [30] Let both grow together until the harvest: and in the time of harvest I will say to the reapers, Gather ye together first the tares, and bind them in bundles to burn them: but gather the wheat into my barn" (Matthew 13:24-30).

"[11] And I saw a great white throne, and him that sat on it, from whose face the earth and the heaven fled away; and there was found no place for them. [12] And I saw the dead, small and great, stand before God; and the books were opened: and another book was opened, which is *the book* of life: and the dead were judged out of those things which were written in the books, according to their works. [13] And the sea gave up the dead which were in it; and death and hell delivered up the dead which were in them: and they were judged every man according to their works. [14] And death and hell were cast into the lake of fire. This is the second death. [15] And whosoever was not found written in the book of life was cast into the lake of fire" (Revelation 20:11-15).

"[1] And at that time shall Michael stand up, the great prince which standeth for the children of thy people: and there shall be a time of trouble, such as never was since there was a nation *even* to that same time: and at that time thy people shall be delivered, every one that shall be found written in the book. [2] And many of them that sleep in the dust of the earth shall awake, some to everlasting life, and some to shame *and* everlasting contempt. [3] And they that be wise shall shine as the brightness of the firmament; and they that turn many to righteousness as the stars for ever and ever" (Daniel 12:1-3).

Handfuls On Purpose
Studies in the Book of Ruth
Chapter Twenty-one
The Resurrection of the Bride of Christ

1. What do Naomi and Ruth typically represent together?

2. Thoroughly explain the following two stages of the oriental marriage.
   A. Kiddushin (Betrothal)
   B. Huppah (bringing the Bride home)

3. Discuss how the above two stages of an oriental wedding relate to the various Eschatological (end time) events of the Church Age. Use Scripture to show the basis of your conclusions.

4. Discuss the difference between the rapture of the Church and the second coming of Christ as they relate to the Bride of Christ.

5. Read I Corinthians 15:1-8. How do the "witnesses" of Ruth 4:11 relate to the witnesses of I Corinthians 15:1-8? What is the theological significance to this comparison?

6. Read Revelation 19:6-9 along with Ruth 4:11-12. How does the oriental wedding custom of a seven-day feast relate to the Marriage Supper of the Lamb in Heaven and the Tribulation time on earth?

7. Read John 3:26-30 along with Revelation 19:6-7. Discuss the friends of the Bridegroom, who they are and how they relate to the "great multitude" of Revelation 19:6.

8. Discuss and explain the three phases of the first resurrection. Give the Scripture you use for the basis of your conclusions.

9. Explain the following Scripture texts according to their Eschatological (end time) chronology (time table).
   A. Matthew 24:29-34
   B. Matthew 13:24-30 along with Revelation 20:11-15 and Daniel 12:1-3

Handfuls On Purpose
Studies in the Book of Ruth
Chapter Twenty-two
The Restoration of the Nation of Israel

"^{14} And the women said unto Naomi, Blessed *be* the LORD, which hath not left thee this day without a kinsman {*redeemer*}, that his name may be famous in Israel. ^{15} And he shall be unto thee a restorer of *thy* life, and a nourisher of thine old age: for thy daughter in law, which loveth thee, which is better to thee than seven sons, hath born him. ^{16} And Naomi took the child, and laid it in her bosom, and became nurse unto it. ^{17} And the women her neighbours gave it a name, saying, There is a son born to Naomi; and they called his name Obed: he *is* the father of Jesse, the father of David. ^{18} Now these *are* the generations of Pharez: Pharez begat Hezron, ^{19} And Hezron begat Ram, and Ram begat Amminadab, ^{20} And Amminadab begat Nahshon, and Nahshon begat **Salmon** {*Salmah*}, ^{21} And Salmon begat Boaz, and Boaz begat Obed, ^{22} And Obed begat Jesse, and Jesse begat David" (Ruth 4:14-22).

Palm Sunday is the day Christians celebrate the triumphant entry of Christ into the city of Jerusalem. However, it was not triumphant. If it had been triumphant, Jesus would have restored the nation of Israel and gathered her together from all the nations of the world. Contrary to the anti-Semitism of Covenant (Reformed) Theology, Christ loves the children of Israel and longs for their salvation and restoration.

"^{34} Wherefore, behold, I send unto you prophets, and wise men, and scribes: and *some* of them ye shall kill and crucify; and *some* of them shall ye scourge in your synagogues, and persecute *them* from city to city: ^{35} That upon you may come all the righteous blood shed upon the earth, from the blood of righteous Abel unto the blood of Zacharias son of Barachias, whom ye slew between the temple and the altar. ^{36} Verily I say unto you, All these things shall come upon this generation. ^{37} <u>O Jerusalem, Jerusalem, *thou* that killest the prophets, and stonest them which are sent unto thee, how often would I have gathered thy children together, even as a hen gathereth her chickens under *her* wings, and ye would not!</u> ^{38} Behold, your house is left unto you desolate. ^{39} For I say unto you, Ye shall not see me henceforth, till ye shall say, Blessed *is* he that cometh in the name of the Lord" (Matthew 23:34-39).

The religious leaders of Judaism rejected the Kingship of Christ, rejecting Him as their Messiah and having Him crucified. By religious leaders of Judaism, it means the "chief priests" and "scribes" of apostate Judaism. Because the priesthood of Israel rejected their promised Messiah, God opened the door for a new priesthood. This new priesthood would be comprised of all who become His children ("whosoever will") from both the nation of Israel and all nations (ethnic groups) of the world.

"[11] He came unto his own, and his own received him not. [12] But as many as received him, to them gave he power to become the sons of God, *even* to them that believe on his name:" (John 1:11-12).

"[17] And Jesus going up to Jerusalem took the twelve disciples apart in the way, and said unto them, [18] Behold, we go up to Jerusalem; and the Son of man shall be betrayed unto the chief priests and unto the scribes, and they shall condemn him to death, [19] And shall deliver him to the Gentiles to mock, and to scourge, and to crucify *him*: and the third day he shall rise again" (Matthew 20:17-19).

When Israel followed their apostate priesthood in the rejection of Jesus the Messiah, God scattered them into every nation of the world through persecution. Although there have been times in history when Israel returned to the Promised Land, in most part they have remained scattered. James addresses his epistle "to the twelve tribes which are scattered abroad (*diaspora*)" (James 1:1). God gave the epistle of James just prior to the dispersion of the Jews and the destruction of the Temple in 70 AD. Therefore, James confirms that God viewed the nation of Israel as still scattered even though they occupied the Promised Land and the Temple.

God has scattered Israel on numerous occasions. The final scattering of Israel was in 70 AD with the destruction of the Temple by the Roman armies of Titus. Israel remains scattered today. God foretold this scattering on numerous occasions and this scattering has been continual. All of the returns of the people of Israel after the dispersion of Nebuchadnezzar (including the present) have only been partial.

"[8] Remember, I beseech thee, the word that thou commandedst thy servant Moses, saying, *If* ye transgress, I will scatter you abroad among the nations: ⁹ But *if* ye turn unto me, and keep my commandments, and do them; though there were of you cast out unto the uttermost part of the heaven, *yet* will I gather them from thence, and will bring them unto the place that I have chosen to set my name there" (Nehemiah 1:8-9; about BC 446).

"¹⁵ Because my people hath forgotten me, they have burned incense to vanity, and they have caused them to stumble in their ways *from* the ancient paths, to walk in paths, *in* a way not cast up; ¹⁶ To make their land desolate, *and* a perpetual hissing; every one that passeth thereby shall be astonished, and wag his head. ¹⁷ I will scatter them as with an east wind before the enemy; I will shew them the back, and not the face, in the day of their calamity" (Jeremiah 18:15-17; about BC 601).

"¹⁴ And I will scatter toward every wind all that *are* about him to help him, and all his bands; and I will draw out the sword after them. ¹⁵ And they shall know that I *am* the LORD, when I shall scatter them among the nations, and disperse them in the countries" (Ezekiel 12:14-15; about BC 594).

Ruth 4:14-15 is in contrast to Ruth 1:19. Ruth 1:19 reveals the fallen state of the nation of Israel.

"So they two went until they came to Bethlehem. And it came to pass, when they were come to Bethlehem, that all the city was moved about them, and they said, *Is* this Naomi" (Ruth 1:19)?

"¹⁴ And the women said unto Naomi, Blessed *be* the LORD, which hath not left thee this day without a kinsman, that his name may be famous in Israel. ¹⁵ And he shall be unto thee a restorer of *thy* life, and a nourisher of thine old age: for thy daughter in law, which loveth thee, which is better to thee than seven sons, hath born him" (Ruth 4:14-15).

The word "restorer" in Ruth 4:15 is a key to what will be happening on earth for those seven years while the Church is celebrating the Marriage Supper of the Lamb in Heaven. God will be restoring the nation of Israel as promised throughout Scripture. Over fifty passages assert the restoration and regathering of Israel *after* the second coming of Christ.

"¹ And it shall come to pass, when all these things are come upon thee, the blessing and the curse, which I have set before thee, and thou shalt call *them* to mind among all the nations, whither the LORD thy God hath driven thee, ² And shalt return unto the LORD thy God, and shalt obey his voice according to all that I command thee this day, thou and thy children, with all thine heart, and with all thy soul; ³ That then the LORD thy God will turn thy captivity, and have compassion upon thee, and will return and gather thee from all the nations, whither the LORD thy God hath scattered thee. ⁴ If *any* of thine be driven out unto the outmost *parts* of heaven, from thence will the LORD thy God gather thee, and from thence will he fetch thee: ⁵ And the LORD thy God will bring thee into the land which thy fathers possessed, and thou shalt possess it; and he will do thee good, and multiply thee above thy fathers. ⁶ And the LORD thy God will circumcise thine heart, and the heart of thy seed, to love the LORD thy God with all thine heart, and with all thy soul, that thou mayest live" (Deuteronomy 30:1-6).

The Scriptures are clear that this regathering will take place *after* the second coming of Christ.

"¹⁶ Moreover, thou son of man, take thee one stick, and write upon it, For Judah, and for the children of Israel his companions: then take another stick, and write upon it, For Joseph, the stick of Ephraim, and *for* all the house of Israel his companions: ¹⁷ And join them one to another into one stick; and they shall become one in thine hand. ¹⁸ And when the children of thy people shall speak unto thee, saying, Wilt thou not shew us what thou *meanest* by these? ¹⁹ Say unto them, Thus saith the Lord GOD; Behold, I will take the stick of Joseph, which *is* in the hand of Ephraim, and the tribes of Israel his fellows, and will put them with him, *even* with the stick of Judah, and make them one stick, and they shall be one in mine hand. ²⁰ And the sticks whereon thou writest shall be in thine hand before their eyes. ²¹ And say unto them, Thus saith the Lord GOD; Behold, I will take the children of Israel from among the heathen, whither they be gone, and will gather them on every side, and bring them into their own land: ²² And I will make them one nation in the land upon the mountains of Israel; and one king shall be king to them all: and they shall be no more two nations, neither shall they be divided into two kingdoms any more at all: ²³ Neither shall they defile themselves any more with their idols, nor with their detestable things, nor with any of their transgressions: but I will save them out of all their dwellingplaces, wherein they have sinned, and will cleanse them: so shall they be my people, and I will be their God. [24] And David my servant *shall be* king over them; and they all shall have one shepherd: they shall also walk in my judgments, and observe my statutes, and do them. [25] And they shall dwell in the land that I have given unto Jacob my servant, wherein your fathers have dwelt; and they shall dwell therein, *even* they, and their children, and their children's children for ever: and my servant David *shall be* their prince for ever. [26] Moreover I will make a covenant of peace with them; it shall be an everlasting covenant with them: and I will place them, and multiply them, and will set my sanctuary in the midst of them for evermore. [27] My tabernacle also shall be with them: yea, I will be their God, and they shall be my people. [28] And the heathen shall know that I the LORD do sanctify Israel, when my sanctuary shall be in the midst of them for evermore" (Ezekiel 37:16-28).

Although the Church is composed of "born again" Jews and Gentiles from the Day of Pentecost to the Rapture, the restoration of the nation of Israel will begin on earth during the Tribulation period. Christ will rule the world from the Throne of David in the city of Jerusalem beginning on the day of His second coming. Although Israel was proclaimed a nation May 14, 1948, *that is not* the fulfillment of the restoration prophecies.

Israel has never reclaimed the Temple and they have not restored the sacrificial offerings. This actual restoration of the nation and regathering of the children of Israel will not happen until the second coming. The Tribulation lays the groundwork for the second advent of Jesus Christ and the establishment of His Kingdom on earth. There will be worldwide national repentance of the Jews on earth at the second coming of Christ.

John the Baptist came preaching, "repent for the kingdom of heaven is at hand" (Matthew 3:2). The nation of Israel as represented in their priesthood refused to repent. In the priesthood's refusal to repent, they rejected their King (that is the pattern consistent with all unbelievers).

"[7] But when he saw many of the Pharisees and Sadducees come to his baptism, he said unto them, O generation of vipers, who hath warned you to flee from the wrath to come? [8] Bring forth therefore fruits meet for repentance: [9] And think not to say within yourselves, We have Abraham to *our* father: for I say unto you, that God is able of these stones to raise up children unto Abraham. ¹⁰ And now also the axe is laid unto the root of the trees: therefore every tree which bringeth not forth good fruit is hewn down, and cast into the fire" (Matthew 3:7-10).

Only one third of the world's population alive on earth at the beginning of the seven-year Tribulation will survive God's judgment of the nations.

"⁷ Awake, O sword, against my shepherd, and against the man *that is* my fellow, saith the LORD of hosts: smite the shepherd, and the sheep shall be scattered: and I will turn mine hand upon the little ones. ⁸ And it shall come to pass, *that* in all the land, saith the LORD, two parts therein shall be cut off *and* die; but the third shall be left therein. ⁹ And I will bring the third part through the fire, and will refine them as silver is refined, and will try them as gold is tried: they shall call on my name, and I will hear them: I will say, It *is* my people: and they shall say, The LORD *is* my God" (Zechariah 13:7-9).

All of the 144,000 Jews that God seals from the twelve tribes of Israel will survive.

"⁴ And I heard the number of them which were sealed: *and there were* sealed an hundred *and* forty *and* four thousand of all the tribes of the children of Israel. ⁵ Of the tribe of Juda *were* sealed twelve thousand. Of the tribe of Reuben *were* sealed twelve thousand. Of the tribe of Gad *were* sealed twelve thousand. ⁶ Of the tribe of Aser *were* sealed twelve thousand. Of the tribe of Nepthalim *were* sealed twelve thousand. Of the tribe of Manasses *were* sealed twelve thousand. ⁷ Of the tribe of Simeon *were* sealed twelve thousand. Of the tribe of Levi *were* sealed twelve thousand. Of the tribe of Issachar *were* sealed twelve thousand. ⁸ Of the tribe of Zabulon *were* sealed twelve thousand. Of the tribe of Joseph *were* sealed twelve thousand. Of the tribe of Benjamin *were* sealed twelve thousand" (Revelation 7:4-8).

"And I looked, and, lo, a Lamb stood on the mount Sion, and with him an hundred forty *and* four thousand, having his Father's name written in their foreheads" (Revelation 14:1).

This remnant of the one third, which has accepted Jesus as their Messiah, constitutes true Israel (Romans 9:6). This is the "all Israel" to which Paul refers in Romans 11:26.

"⁶ Not as though the word of God hath taken none effect. For they *are* not all Israel, which are of Israel: ⁷ Neither, because they are the seed of Abraham, *are they* all children: but, In Isaac shall thy seed be called. ⁸ That is, They which are the children of the flesh, these *are* not the children of God: but the children of the promise are counted for the seed" (Romans 9:6-8).

"²⁵ For I would not, brethren, that ye should be ignorant of this mystery, lest ye should be wise in your own conceits; that blindness in part is happened to Israel, until the fulness of the Gentiles be come in. ²⁶ And so <u>all Israel</u> shall be saved: as it is written, There shall come out of Sion the Deliverer, and shall turn away ungodliness from Jacob: ²⁷ For this *is* my covenant unto them, when I shall take away their sins" (Romans 11:25-27).

Today, the focus of the world remains on a seemingly small and insignificant nation in the Middle East called Israel. This nation is comprised of a people who have miraculously survived by God's protection as the world continues to attempt to annihilate them. God has made a promise to the nation of Israel and God keeps His promises. God will restore and regather the nation of Israel just as His Word says.

Yet, like God's conditions on all men, only those who repent and believe will be saved. God's goodness patiently continues to lead men to repent and believe.

"The Lord is not slack concerning his promise, as some men count slackness; but is longsuffering to us-ward, not willing that any should perish, but that all should come to repentance" (II Peter 3:9).

Handfuls On Purpose
Studies in the Book of Ruth
Chapter Twenty-two
The Restoration of the Nation of Israel

1. Discuss why the so-called Triumphal Entry into Jerusalem (Luke 19:28-40) was not triumphal.

2. Read Matthew 23:34-39. What does this portion of Scripture reveal about Christ's attitude toward the nation of Israel?

3. Read John 1:11-12. What is the significance of theses verses involving the first advent of Christ and the "whosoever will" of Romans 10:13?

4. Read James 1:1. What is the significance of this statement compared to the fact that Israel still occupied the Temple and a portion of the Land at the time of this writing?

5. Read Nehemiah 1:8-9, Jeremiah 18:15-17, and Ezekiel 12:14-15. Discuss the significance of these verses as they relate to the nation of Israel's position before God today.

6. Read Ruth 4:15. Discuss the theological significance of the word "restorer" as it relates to the future promise of God to Israel.

7. Read Deuteronomy 30:1-6. Discuss the relevant issues relating to the restoration and regathering of Israel as revealed in this text.

8. Read Ezekiel 37:16-28. Discuss the relevant issues relating to the restoration and regathering of Israel as revealed in this text.

9. Why can we be sure that May 14, 1948 (when Israel was once again proclaimed a nation) is not the fulfillment of the prophecies about the restoration and regathering?

10. Read Zechariah 13:7-9. Discuss the significance of this prophecy to the restoration and regathering of the nation of Israel.

11. Read Romans 9:6-8 and 11:25-27. Discuss the significance of these Scriptures as they relate to the restoration and regathering of Israel.

Lexicons and Dictionaries

Kittel, Gerhard and Gerhard Friedrich, Editors.
Theological Dictionary of the New Testament, Ten Volumes
Translated and edited by Geoffrey W. Bromiley.
Wm. B. Eerdmans Publishing Co., reprinted September 1983.

Richards, Lawrence O.
Expository Dictionary of Bible Words
Regency Reference Library
Zondervan Publishing House, 1985.

Thayer, Joseph H.
Thayer's Greek English Lexicon of the New Testament
Baker Book House, Fifth Printing March 1980.

Tenney, Merrill C., General Editor.
The Zondervan Pictoral Encyclopedia of the Bible, Five Volumes
Associate Editor: Steven Barabas
Zondervan Publishing House, Fifth Printing 1982.

Unger, Merrill F.
The New Unger's Bible Dictionary
Edited by R.K. Harrison, Howard F. Vos and Cyril J. Barber contributing editors.
Moody Press, Revised and updated 1988.

Vine, W. E.
An Expository Dictionary of New Testament Words
Fleming H. Revell Company, Seventeenth impression, 1966.

The Online Bible 7.0, Deluxe Edition.

SwordSearcher Software. Deluxe Version 6.2.1.

www.ingramcontent.com/pod-product-compliance
Lightning Source LLC
Chambersburg PA
CBHW071706090426
42738CB00009B/1680